Kahal Kadosh Beth Elohim (Charleston, S.C.)

Hymns Written For the Use of Hebrew Congregations

Kahal Kadosh Beth Elohim (Charleston, S.C.)

Hymns Written For the Use of Hebrew Congregations

ISBN/EAN: 9783744776776

Printed in Europe, USA, Canada, Australia, Japan

Cover: Foto ©Lupo / pixelio.de

More available books at **www.hansebooks.com**

HYMNS

WRITTEN

FOR THE USE

OF

HEBREW CONGREGATIONS.

"I will sing unto the Lord while I live: I will sing praise unto my God while I exist." PSALM CIV., V. 33.

Fourth Edition, Revised and Corrected.

CHARLESTON, S. C.
PUBLISHED BY THE
CONGREGATION BETH ELOHIM.
A. M. 5627.

Entered according to Act of Congress, in the year 1856, by the Hebrew Congregation
BETH ELOHIM,
In the Clerk's office of the District Court of the United States, for the District of South Carolina.

CHARLESTON, S. C.
EDWARD PERRY, PRINTER,
149 MEETING STREET.—1875.

INDEX OF SUBJECTS.

	Hymns
I. CONSECRATION HYMNS	1—3
II. ATTRIBUTES OF GOD.	
1. Unity of God	4—5
2. Immutability of God	6
3. Omnipotence	7—8
4. Omniscience	9—11
5. Omnipresence	12—13
6. Divine Love	14
7. Divine Mercy	15—19
8. Divine Providence	20—22
9. Divine Providence in relation to Israel	23—26
III. THE DIGNITY AND DESTINY OF MAN.	
1. Man's Dignity	27
2. Man, the Image of God	28
3. Virtue	29—30
4. Piety	31—38
5. Immortality of the Soul	39—43
6. Commemoration of the Dead	44—45

	Hymns.

IV. RELATION BETWEEN GOD AND MAN.

1. Revelation.. 46
2. Divine Law..................................... 47
3. Religion.. 48–51
4. Duties towards God.
    1. Acquisition of the Knowledge of the Lord........................... 52
    2. Obedience to the Will of God........ 53–56
    3. Faith in God................................. 57–60
    4. Hope in God................................. 61–64
    5. Love of God.................................. 65
    6. Gratitude towards God................. 66–67
    7. Submission to the Will of God..... 68–81
5. Duties towards Ourselves.
    1. Self-knowledge............................. 82
    2. Self-examination.......................... 83–85
    3. Humility....................................... 86–89
    4. Contentment................................ 90–94
    5. For the Sick................................. 95
    6. Preparation for Death.................. 96
6. Duties towards Others.
    1. Truth... 97—98
    2. Honesty....................................... 99
    3. Justice... 100
    4. Righteousness............................. 101
    5. Forbearance................................ 102–105
    6. Brotherly Love............................. 106–108
    7. Filial Love................................... 109–110
    8. Matrimonial Love........................ 111
    9. Charity.. 112–119

V. MISCELLANEOUS HYMNS.

1. Faith, Hope, and Love..................... 120
2. Prayer... 121–124

INDEX OF SUBJECTS.

		Hymns.
3.	Divine Worship	125–127
4.	Devotion	128–129
5.	Praise and Thanksgiving	130–141
6.	Morning	142
7.	Evening	143
8.	Spring	144
9.	Winter	145–146
10.	Peace	147–148
11.	Our Country	149
12.	Penitence	150–163

VI. SABBATH HYMNS 164–177

VII. FESTIVAL HYMNS.

1.	New Year (Roshe Hashanah)	178–181
2.	Day of Atonement (Yome Hakippureem)	182–186
3.	Tabernacles (Succoth)	187–191
4.	Feast of Dedication (Hanuccah)	192–194
5.	Feast of Esther (Pureem)	195–196
6.	Passover (Pesach)	197–201
7.	Pentecost (Shabungoth)	202–204

VIII. CONFIRMATION HYMNS 205–207

APPENDIX.

SCHOOL HYMNS 208–210
HEBREW HYMNS ..... pages 210–212

INDEX OF FIRST LINES.

	Number.	Page.
ABOVE all honor and all praise	137	135
Affliction cometh not from dust	73	74
All living souls shall bless Thy name	136	134
Almighty God! Thy special grace	195	190
Almighty God! we pray to Thee	210	209
Almighty God! whose will alone	11	15
A mournful lament for the dead	41	44
Arise! let the souls of the Hebrews rejoice	194	189
BEFORE the glorious orbs of light	4	7
Begin the holy hymn of praise	129	127
Between the past and future year	178	171
Blest are th' enlight'ners of mankind	50	53
Blest is the bond of wedded love	111	110
Blest is the man to whom the Lord	35	39
Bounteous Father! by what course	115	113
By Babel's streams Thy children wept	2	5
CAST me not from Thy presence, Lord	158	154
Comfort ye, O Israel! and lift no more	186	180
Creator of the universe	163	158

INDEX OF FIRST LINES.

	Number.	Page.
DAUGHTERS of Israel! arise	165	160
Deep silence reigned in Isaac's tent	56	58
Descend into thyself, my soul	83	83
Despond not, O my heart	76	76
Divine Disposer of events	10	14
Draw nigh, O Lord! unto my soul	70	71
EARLY and late my God I seek	98	96
Eternal, almighty, invisible God	133	131
Eternal love is Thine, O God	184	178
Exalted theme of human praise	156	151
Extol the King who, throned above	135	133
Exult, my soul! in consciousness proud	28	33
FATHER of mercies! on this morning	185	178
Father of nations! Judge divine	149	144
Father! will abstinence, or prayer, or song	99	97
Fear not, fear not, O Jeshurun	25	30
Formless and void creation stood	53	56
Frail, feeble, inefficient man	80	80
From my voice shall virtue's praise proceed	157	152
GATHER and worship! the first star of eve	164	159
Glorified throughout all time	7	11
Glory and praise to the bountiful Sire	138	135
Glory not in a gift so vain	52	54
Glory to God! whose outstretched hand	200	196
God dwells in light	193	188
God of my fathers! in Thy sight	207	205
God of my fathers! merciful and just	39	43
God of power! in Thy gift	29	34
God of the earth, the air, the sea	197	192
God of the Sabbath! to Thy praise	170	163
God of the universe! unfailing friend	79	79

INDEX TO FIRST LINES.

	Number.	Page.
God Supreme! to Thee I pray	68	70
God! to my spirit's great delight	205	202
Great Arbiter of human fate	192	186
HALLELUJAH! praise to Thee	199	195
Hallelujah	201	197
Hallow my Sabbaths! Will Israel respond	174	167
Happy he whom nature mouldeth	206	204
Have mercy on Thy servant, Lord	151	147
Healer of the wounded heart	74	75
Hearken not, man! to the voice of self-love	86	86
Hear my voice and grant my pray'r	95	94
Here at this temple's holy shrine	127	125
He spoke; and through the gloom profound	167	161
Holy and everlasting One	144	141
House of Judah, bless the Lord	139	136
How beautiful it is to see	106	104
How cold that man! to faith how dead	20	24
How desolate thy fields and vales	187	181
How great, how pure is my delight	191	185
How long will man, in pleasure merged	32	37
How oft has man, with "heart of stone"	119	117
How sad the wintry hours seem	146	142
I LIFT mine eyes unto the hills	61	63
I saw a palace proud and high	113	111
I tremble not; Thou, Lord, art nigh	13	17
I weep not now as once I wept	57	59
I wept when from my eager grasp	71	72
I will extol Thee, O my King	19	23
I will still remain with Thee	21	25
If mortal vision may not meet	140	137
In glory, Lord! dost Thou appear	85	85
In God, the holy, wise, and just	9	13

n harmony with heaven's peace	171
n holiness, eternal Lord	34
n perilous probation here	124
n the great scales of human life	90
ntensely radiant was thy peak	110
nto the tomb of ages past	179
s there within the world's wide bound	148
srael! to holy numbers	3
t is the solemn Sabbath-day	166
EADERS of Israel! arise	152
et choral songs of gladness flow	46
et me for present hours borrow	93
et the Lord be ever praised	131
et the standard of truth by Judah be planted	97
et there be love! it is the light	107
et thy heart for ever delight in the Lord	59
et us to prayer; it is the holy time	202
ift, lift the voice of praise on high	126
o! He sleeps and slumbers not	24
ook down, O God! with gracious eye	181
ord! let Thy countenance now shine	75
ord! my Redeemer and my Rock	38
ord of the world! when I behold	183
ord! what is man, that Thou shouldst take	51
ord! when I hear Thy holy law	47
AN of the world! wilt thou not pause	33
any are the pains and sorrows	77
orn breaks upon Moriah's height	180
ournfully chant! for our choir accords	160
y God, my Father, and my Guide	89
y God! my God! to Thee I cling	81
y heart is bared to Thee, O Lord	182

INDEX OF FIRST LINES.

	Number.	Page.
NOT for affliction, gracious God	14	19
Now let the hand of toil suspend	172	165
O'ER all this wide and beauteous earth	17	22
Of all the virtues that we find	102	100
Of heaven's bounties let us sing	190	184
O God! as we on nature gaze	6	9
O God! to-day our joyful song of praise	196	191
O God! to Thy paternal grace	58	60
O God! within Thy temple walls	27	32
Oh! answer me, my God! this day	150	146
Oh! blest be he who ne'er forgets the poor	116	114
Oh! ever adverse to the scheme	103	101
Oh! fill our hearts, almighty King	208	208
Oh! how imperfect, blind, and false	36	40
Oh! how shall man with God contend	54	57
Oh! let us mingle heart and voice	198	193
Oh! love the Lord with all thy heart	65	67
Oh! plaintive be the touch and tone	162	157
Oh! sad is nature's aspect now	145	141
Oh! that on morning's dewy wings	69	71
Oh! turn at meek devotion's call	31	36
Oh! what avails my destination	30	35
Oh! whence doth human happiness arise	91	90
Oh! where is he who yesterday	94	93
Oh! worship God! approach His shrine	125	123
Oh! worship not at glory's shrine	154	150
O King of glory! when we contemplate	16	21
O man! frail child of finite pow'rs	44	47
On dim futurity with idle aim	92	91
One God! One Lord! One mighty King	5	8
On Shinar's plain see Babel's tower rise	88	88
O Thou! in whom the power dwells	72	73
O thou! possest of health and bloom	96	94

INDEX OF FIRST LINES.

xi

	Number.	Page.
O Thou! who, as the great Unknown	147	143
O Thou! who dwell'st in heights supernal	45	48
O Thou! whose shrine the sweetest incense bears	112	110
O uncreated Holy One	132	130
Out of sorrow's depths I cry	87	87
PRAISE the Counselor supreme	188	182
Praise the Lord God, the glorious Supreme	173	166
Praise to the God of nations sing	177	170
Praise ye the Lord! for it is good	130	128
Pray in the night, when silence and the stars	118	116
Pray when the morn unveileth	121	119
Prepare and purify my heart	175	168
Princes of earth, bend lowly down	141	138
REBUKE me not, nor chasten me	60	62
Refreshed by sleep, that sovereign balm	142	139
Refuge I seek at the shrine of devotion	128	126
Rejoice in God, our mighty Rock	203	200
Remember, man, while thou art young	49	52
Rest for the Lord! The work is done	176	169
Return, O Lord! and let me be	114	112
Rude are the tabernacles now	189	183
SOURCE of Mercy, Truth, and Grace	168	162
Stranger to that pure ambition	159	154
Stretched languidly upon his couch	117	115
THE heavens, Almighty! Thy glory declare	37	41
The Lord, a watchful guardian, reigns	143	140
The Lord of heaven reigns	8	12
The prophet to the people said	100	98
The sun shines on with glorious light	23	28
Though faith's discordant worshipers may rear	123	121
Though I from kindred meet but scorn	62	64

INDEX OF FIRST LINES.

	Number.	Page.
Though man of all the ruin hears	42	45
Though sorrows may be multiplied	55	57
To man, with reason's gift endued	67	69
To smile when we on life's breakers are tossed	48	51
Through the valley of tears as we thoughtfully	43	46
Truly and tenderly should I	108	106
UNLESS the land where ye abide	26	31
Unto Thine altar, King of kings	155	150
WE bless Thee, O Lord! as the bountiful Source	134	132
We bring not to our holy shrine	204	201
We look to Thee, ineffable King	22	27
Weeping, and loth from all she loved to part	18	22
What cause hast thou, O Israel! for tears	105	103
What painful mem'ries from the buried past	153	149
When Faith, too young for a sublimer creed	1	3
When grief on the heart has weighed	64	66
When I remember, O my God	109	108
When I would smile, remembrance brings	78	78
When light broke forth at God's command	15	20
When morning paints the eastern sky	40	44
When night from nature's kingdom flies	122	120
Wherefore Hallelujah sing	12	16
While man explores with curious eye	82	82
Who, God of glory! shall be found	101	99
Who is that angel of the universe	120	118
Why art thou cast down, my soul	63	65
Why, O heedless mortal! dost thou fly	84	84
Why, O man! is not thy soul's desire	104	102
With ardent love and reverence deep	66	68
With grateful hearts of song and praise	209	208
With joyful heart I greet again	169	163
Woe unto Zion! she is spoiled	161	156

HYMNS.

HYMNS.

1. CONSECRATION HYMNS.*

1 1 When Faith, too young for a sublimer creed,
  Her simple text from nature's volume taught,
She 'wakened Melody, whose shell and reed,
  Though rude, upon her spirit gently
    wrought.
But soon from sylvan altars she took wing,
  And music followed still the angel's flight;
Savage no more, she touched a golden string,
  And sung of God, in Revelation's light.
    Lend, lend our chords, ye seraph-pair,
      The soul of Jesse's son,
    That we may in harmonious prayer,
      Exalt the Holy One!

* Hymns 1, 2, and 3 were sung at the consecration of the Synagogue of the Congregation Beth Elohim, on Friday, the 26th of Adar, A. M., 5601.

2 Girt in His lightning robe, God gave the law,
   From trembling Sinai, to His eldest-born;
Tablets, that time from memory could not draw,
   A talisman in Judah's bosom worn.
      His spirit before thousands past,
        To *one* alone revealed;
      And 'mid the thunder's awful blast,
        Faith's covenant was sealed.

3 "Him first, Him last," Him let us ever sing,
   Whose promise yet the Hebrew pilgrim cheers;
Who shall His wandering people once more bring
   Back to the glory of departed years.
      Bright pillar of our desert path,
        Through shame and scorn adored;
      Thy mercy triumph's o'er thy wrath,
        Creator, King, and Lord!

4 Lost is the pomp, that in the land of palms
   Thy regal temple on Moriah graced;
No wreathing incense *here* Thy shrine embalms,
   No cherub-plumes are round its altars placed.
      Our censer is the "vital urn,"
        Our ark's upborne by zeal;
      To these, Almighty! wilt thou turn
        At Israel's appeal.

5 Now, let joyous Hallelujah's ring,
   The *fallen* casts her ashes far away;
Behold another fane from ruin spring,
   In brighter and more beautiful array.

>   Enter in brotherly accord
>   God's holy dwelling-place;
>   Chastened in spirit and in word,
>   There supplicate His grace.

6 Hear, O Supreme! our humble invocation,
    Our country, kindred, and the stranger
        bless!
Bless, too, this sanctuary's consecration,
    Its hallowed purpose on our hearts impress.
        Still, still let choral harmony
            Ascend before Thy throne;
        While echoing seraphim reply:
            The Lord our God is One!   P. M.

COMFORT YE! COMFORT YE!

Isaiah, chap. XL., v. 1.

1 By Babel's streams Thy children wept;
    Then mute, O Israel! was thy choir;
While as thy weary exiles slept,
    And on the willow hung thy lyre,
        A seraph's voice, soft as the dew,
            Fell on their dream with "Nahamoo."

2 No song made glad that mournful voice;
    No ease was for that bruised breast,
'Till He who led thee to rejoice,
    Sent forth from Zion His behest!
        Firm as thy faith in Him was true,
        Like manna fell the "Nahamoo."

3 The stranger hath usurped the seat
    Where, crowned with glory, blaz'd thy fane

"The flow'ry brooks thy hallow'd feet
  Still wash," O Zion! still remain
    To mark the ruin and renew
    The memory of the "Nahamoo."

4 God's mercies shine, a lingering beam,
    The pilgrim on his path to light;
  From Sinai's brow, from Jordan's stream,
    From off'rings of the heart contrite,
      His promises all our hopes imbue
      With blessings of the "Nahamoo."

J. C. L.

3

1 Israel! to holy numbers
    Tune thy harp's exalting strain;
  From its long entranced slumbers
    Wake to life its soul again.

2 Give to song its ancient glories,
    Let the pealing anthems rise,
  Proudly to rehearse the stories—
    Gem'd with glory from the skies.

3 Gently chaunt fair Miriam's praise,
    Faith sustained her heart sincere;
  'Twas *her* first enraptured lays,
    Sounding timbrils tuned to prayer.

4 Rejoicing went the welcome song,
    As to heaven up it rose,
  Sweet spirits would the sound prolong,
    Half awak'ning from repose.

5 Almighty God! before this shrine
    Man his Maker worships free;
  Oh! bless it with Thy love divine,
    Fill it with Thy charity.

6 God is eternal—and alone!
    Humbly let us bend the knee,
While seraph's guard His sacred throne,
    Linking immortality.   C. M.

II. ATTRIBUTES OF GOD.

1. UNITY OF GOD.

(ADONE NGOLAM.)

1 Before the glorious orbs of light
    Had shed one blissful ray,
In awful power the Lord of might
    Reigned in eternal day.

2 At His creative, holy word,
    The voice of nature spoke;
Unnumber'd worlds, with one accord,
    To living joys awoke.

3 Then was proclaimed the mighty King,
    In majesty on high;
Then did the holy creatures sing
    His praises through the sky.

4 All merciful in strength he reigns,
    Immutable, Supreme;
His hand the universe sustains,
    He only can redeem.

5 He is the mighty God alone,
    His presence fills the world;
He will forever reign, the One,
    Eternal, only Lord!

6 Almighty, powerful and just,
   Thou art my God, my friend!
My rock, my refuge, and my trust,
   On Thee my hopes depend.

7 Oh! be my guardian whilst I sleep,
   For thou didst lend me breath;
And when I wake my spirit keep,
   And save my soul in death.   D. N. C.

5

1 One God! One Lord! One mighty King!
   In unity will Judah sing;
Transmitting e'er from sire to son
The truth that God is only One.

2 Thee, Sov'reign of the universe,
Through ages, 'mid all sects diverse,
The Hebrew child is taught to praise,
To lisp Thy name, and learn Thy ways.

3 To Thee alone, when life recedes,
The dying Israelite still pleads;
In *One* Redeemer, God, and guide
His fleeting spirit doth confide.

4 Centre and Source of truth sublime!
The sun is but a lamp of time,
A transient spark by mercy fed,
That man might up to Thee be led.

5 Thy law is that eternal Light,
That dawning first on Horeb's height,
Still deigns on Israel to shine,
A proof of grace and love divine.

6 It penetrates the stubborn heart,
And purifies its sinful part.

The voice of God, O Judah! hear,
And fix His law for ever there.   P. M.

2. IMMUTABILITY OF GOD.

Psalm xc.

6 1 O God! as we on nature gaze,
    We see through all her mighty maze,
      The spirit of mutation;
    Thou art alone with power endued
    To triumph o'er vicissitude;
      Thou knowest no variation.
        Stars disappear
        From heaven's sphere,
        Yet *Thou* art there!
        Seas shrink to rills,
        High rocks to hills;
    Such change but nature's law fulfills.

   2 Exhaustless Source of countless suns!
     Thy voice to earth's unheeding ones
       This mandate e'er resoundeth:
     Alike ye abject and august,
     Sink, downward sink, to kindred dust,
       Where death his empire foundeth.
         God of the spheres!
         A thousand years
         One day appears
         To Thee, whose hand
         The heavens spanned,
     And worlds on worlds stupendous planned.

   3 We are as flowers of the mead,
     Bearing corruption's fatal seed
       Within our heart's recesses;

But, oh! believe the truth we sing,
To soul and blossom comes a spring,
   That vivifies and blesses.
      Each hath its tears,
      Each tribute bears
      Of sweets or prayers,
      But man, whose mind
      God's image shrined,
Shall place among immortals find.

4 Behold the grass with dew-drops decked!
Canst thou in its green spires detect
   Aught that decay portendeth?
Yet look, at eve, on each young blade
That in the beams of morning played,
   Cut down—with dust it blendeth.
      Type of man's fate!
      With youth elate
      His mortal date
      Remote appears:
      'Till waning years
Wither the verdure life first bears.

5 Three-score—how small a part is this,
Of ages cast in that abyss
   Where time his victims hideth;
That tomb of *many yesterdays*,
From which a voice proceeds and says
   To those whom reason guideth:
      From this our grave,
      Ye fair and brave,
      Your *morrows* save
      Lest by neglect
      These two are wrecked,
And buried 'neath oblivion's wave.

6 Then count the moments as they pass,
   Shining or dark, from time's sand-glass,
     Ere they depart for ever;
  From each some blessed thought extract,
  To each attach some godly act,
     Or virtuous endeavor.
        Then shall no change
        Your peace derange,
        Your souls estrange
        From that great guide
        Who rules the tide,
That past from future doth divide.

7 Immutability is Thine,
  Creator, King, and Lord divine,
    In whom perfection dwelleth!
  Oh! bring us nearer to Thy throne,
  Let us from angels catch the tone
     That of thy glory telleth.
        Oh! bless the meek
        Who daily seek
        Thy praise to speak;
        Whose efforts blend,
        Faith to extend
  In Thee, man's never-changing Friend!
P. M.

3. OMNIPOTENCE.

7 1 Glorified throughout all time,
    Be the name of God supreme!
  Who in heaven reigned sublime,
    Ere creation felt His beam.

  2 He the world's foundation laid
    By His strength of will alone;

Suns and stars around him played,
 Catching splendor from His throne.

3 Nature, at His bidding, brought
 Atoms into elements;
Works of beauty then were wrought,
 Worthy of Omnipotence.

4 Mountains towered high and vast,
 Seas from viewless caverns gushed,
Infant winds serenely passed,
 Flowers into being blushed.

5 Tenants of the air and deep,
 Animals that tread the ground,
Insect tribes that o'er it creep,
 Were to life and order bound.

6 Man, at last, God's spirit felt
 Glowing warmly in his soul;
Earth before a sov'reign knelt,
 And acknowledged his control.

7 With this spark of light divine,
 Shining o'er the breast within,
Mortal, oh! what shame is thine,
 When thou fallest into sin.

8 1 The Lord of heaven reigns,
 Eternal and sublime;
All limit he disdains
 Of power, space, or time.

2 Though ages take their flight,
 No change in Him it makes,
Whose raiment is the light,
 Whose voice in thunder speaks.

3 Stars with His essence fraught,
  In harmony unite,
To praise the Hand that wrought
  The orbs of day and night.

4 As ocean ebbs and flows,
  Swayed by its viewless guide,
In tempest or repose,
  God still is glorified.

5 O Lord! let me not fail
  In trials of the soul;
Let perfect faith prevail,
  And pious self-control.

6 Desert not Thy frail charge,
  But with a father's care
My heart and mind enlarge,
  To *bear* and to *forbear*.   P. M.

4. OMNISCIENCE.

9 1 In God, the holy, wise, and just,
     From childhood's tender years,
   Have I reposed with perfect trust
     My worldly hopes and fears.

2 From every page that time has turned,
    Since that bright season fled,
  Some useful lesson have I learned,
    Some striking moral read.

3 The prize ambition keenly sought,
    A worthless bauble proved;
  The web of gold by av'rice wrought,
    A mighty Hand removed.

4 No self-exalting scheme can man,
    Unknown to God, project;
No dark device the sland'rer plan,
    Which He will not detect.

5 In vain would evil-doers hope
    His scrutiny to fly;
Nought passes beneath heaven's cope,
    Unnoticed by His eye.

6 Oh! should my term of life exceed
    Frail man's allotted days,
In age to Mercy would I plead
    For strength my God to praise.   P. M.

10

1 Divine Disposer of events!
    To whom all praise belongs;
Each attribute of Thine presents
    A theme for countless songs.

2 Though mortal years were multiplied
    A thousand thousand fold;
Yet time would scarcely be supplied,
    Thy powers to unfold.

3 How shall a feeble, finite mind
    Of Thine omniscience sing?
Wisdom for this no words can find,
    And melody no string.

4 In timid tones if angels speak
    Of Thee, all-knowing God!
How then shall man, minute and weak,
    Thy excellencies laud?

5 All heights and depths in nature's bound
    Are visible to Thee,

The lofty heart, the mind profound,
　The mountain and the sea.

6　No eye but Thine, eternal King!
　　Can penetrate the grave;
　No hand but Thine from thence can bring
　　The soul Thy grace will save.

7　Oh! let us then in virtue's scale
　　Strive ever to ascend,
　And find, beyond this tearful vale,
　　An everlasting Friend.　　　P. M.

GENESIS, CHAP. XVI., V. 13.

11　1　Almighty God! whose will alone
　　Sufficed the world to fabricate;
　Whose comprehensive glance is thrown
　　O'er every empire, realm and state:
　How from Thy ever-searching eye,
　　Can man the *heart's* dominion hide?
　Where passions among virtues lie,
　　As reptiles among flowers glide.

2　Father of mercies! aid my soul
　　Its failings to eradicate;
　Let truth its every thought control,
　　Its every feeling elevate.
　Fearless before Thee let me stand,
　　O Lord! in conscious rectitude;
　And feel, when human deeds are scanned,
　　That mine with favor shall be viewed.
　　　　　　　　　　　　　P. M.

5. OMNIPRESENCE.

12 1 Wherefore Hallelujah sing,
    O thou who knowest not
Where an omnipresent King
    May by thy soul be sought?
Canst thou fix the point or place
    That His spirit holdeth?
Earth and heaven, time and space,
    In His grasp He foldeth.

2 Dust-born atom! look above,
    Where lustrous worlds are shrined;
Ask, if all-pervading Love,
    To these His light confined?
Let proud ocean's voice attest,
    (Though fathomless to man,)
If ubiquity may rest
    Within its mighty span.

3 Ask of the blast that rendeth
    The forest's sylvan robe,
Whether it comprehendeth
    The Ruler of the globe?
Turn from living elements
    To those by death dissolved;
Ever-present Providence!
    Art Thou in these involved?

4 All repeat as they respond:
    "What can the *boundless* hold?"
Answered from the world beyond:
    "Naught of a finite mould!"
Yet by whirlwinds, stars and seas,
    The Lord is magnified;
Shall not *human* praise then please
    Our omnipresent Guide?

5 Oh! then let no emotion
    By which the heart is swayed,
Prevent that deep devotion,
    That should to God be paid.
Social life and solitude
    Alike shall prompt the prayer,
That faith, hope, and gratitude
    Before His throne shall bear.   P. M.

13
1 I tremble not! Thou, Lord, art nigh,
    All-knowing and all-seeing!
To *Thee*, disconsolate, I fly,
    Kind Guardian of my being.
From infancy to age mature,
Thee only did my soul adore.

2 To ev'ry evil that annoys,
    To every trial fearful,
Thou bringest some light counterpoise,
    To make earth's vale less tearful.
But, oh! how few interpret right,
Either the blessing or the blight.

3 Sad consciousness have I, alas!
    Of sinful meditation;
O'er which Omniscience cannot pass
    Without stern reprobation.
Yet doubt shall not my faith debase,
That sets no limit to Thy grace.

4 Self-kindled, Thine intelligence
    The universe enlightens;
And darkness, e'en the most intense,
    To mid-day splendor brightens.
Guilt vainly seeks nocturnal shades,
Since naught Thy mighty grasp evades.

5 A sinner's cry, a seraph's call,
   Alternate Thou attendest;
A flower's rise, an empire's fall,
   In one survey Thou blendest.
All nature 'neath Thy glance expands,
But who *Thine* essence understands?

6 "Show me Thy glory?" said the seer,
   Who Sinai's law attested;
"In graciousness will I appear
   Before Thee manifested."
Thus did the voice of God proclaim,—
Goodness and glory were the same.

7 Invisibly He passeth by
   His children every hour,
Who from devotion's rock descry
   His majesty and power;
But none among the living seen
May contemplate His awful mien.

8 Yet through my spirit, oft I see
   His countenance all beaming;
When charity, by His decree,
   Worth is from want redeeming.
And man, most like his Maker, shows
When this pure love within him glows.

9 I tremble not my heart to bare
   Before Thee, Judge eternal!
Whose hand will dry contrition's tear,
   With tenderness paternal.
Whose mercy hath to mortals given
Promise and foretaste of Thy heaven.

P. M.

6. DIVINE LOVE.

14

1 Not for affliction, gracious God!
   Sons of dust didst Thou create
Blossoms on Thy penal rod,
   Its keen strokes to mitigate.

2 Buds of joy and thorns of sorrow
   On the tree of life arise;
Care to-day, content to-morrow,
   Thus human lot diversifies.

3 Upon the verge of midnight's skies,
   Dawn's silver herald gleams;
So hope, that on grief's border lies,
   The heart from gloom redeems.

4 And as night's silence, deep and drear,
   By morning's voice is broken,
So is the stillness of despair,
   By words that faith had spoken.

5 Winter, inclement and unkind,
   Yet guards the sleeping flowers,
That spring on its return may find
   These smiling in her bowers.

6 Adversity's most bitter day
   From us *this* world estrangeth;
But for the soul prepares the way
   To one that never changeth.

7 The thunder-clouds of war contain
   Elements of peace serene,
That brings a rainbow back again,
   Where martial storm had been.

8 Meek faith converts the couch of pain
   Into a bed of roses;

For there we moral vigor gain,
  To bear what God disposes.

9 The soul there breaks it carnal shell,
  Impatient for that station
Where saints and seraphs ever dwell,—
  The kingdom of salvation.

10 A God, a Father, holds the scale
  That good and ill comprises;
Oh! then let trust in *Him* prevail,
  Which e'er of these arises.   P. M.

7. DIVINE MERCY.

GENESIS, CHAP. IX., v. 13.

15 1 When light broke forth at God's command,
It brightened ocean, air and land,
'Twas then that clouds, and shells, and flowers
Caught vivid colors from its showers.

2 But soon the earth waxed bold in guilt,
Defiling shrines by virtue built;
Proud man pursued his evil course,
Unchecked by reason or remorse.

3 No ray of light creation cheered;
Skies black as mortal sin appeared;
Then burst the deluge o'er the doomed,
And wrath divine a *world* entombed.

4 Behold! upon the wings of light,
Tremble the rain-drops large and bright;
And, lo! the tears of recent storm
Have taken Mercy's radiant form.

5 The bow, the covenant, the token,
 The promise never to be broken,
 Expands in beauty o'er the sod,
 Where Noah rears a shrine to God.

P. M.

16
1 O King of glory! when we contemplate
 Thy majesty and our mean estate;
 Thy purity, that by the angels seen,
 Makes even *their* bright spirits seem unclean.
 How wondrously benign dost Thou appear,
 O'er mortals to extend a *Father's* care!

2 Oh! were it not for mercy such as Thine,
 How could the conscious sinner seek Thy shrine?
 How hope for grace, when long arrears of sin
 Recorded stand upon the soul within?
 But Thou, O Lord! with clemency divine,
 Wilt not the guilty to despair consign.

3 *Who* more than Judah can this truth attest?
 To *whom* hath goodness been more manifest?
 Though from the prophet's harp he proudly turned,
 And inspiration's warning music spurned;
 Through ages he to Heaven's promise clings,
 And far from Zion of salvation sings.

4 Beneath the pressure of a thousand ills,
 One hope the heart of every Hebrew thrills,
 That he may yet prove worthy of Thy love,
 And by repentance ling'ring wrath remove;
 The frown of Justice change to Mercy's smile,
 Blest as an Israelite devoid of guile.

P. M.

17
1 O'er all this wide and beauteous earth,
   One God immortal reigns—
  His glory, truth, and unity
   Link'd by eternal chains.

2 Let angels join in holy song,
   Around His heav'nly throne;
  And mortals, with undying hope,
   Look up to Him alone.

3 The gratitude of ev'ry heart
   Its incense bears to Thee,
  O Ruler of the starry sky,
   The earth and boundless sea!

4 Thy mercy shines divinely bright,
   A mild, yet glowing beam,
  And ev'ry soul that worships Thee,
   In love wilt Thou redeem.

5 Thy blessings fall like morning dews,
   To cheer each troubled breast;
  Thy presence o'er the universe
   For ever is confessed.

6 'Tis Thou canst calm the angry waves,
   And still the tempest's roar,
  Almighty God! whose glory gilds
   Eternity's bright shore.   C. M. C.

GENESIS, CHAP. XXI.

18
1 Weeping, and loth from all she loved to part,
   Stood Hagar, trembling at her Lord's decree;
  And, oh! how like a desert was her heart,
   When from His gentle presence urged to flee.

2 But Sarah's looks, full of indignant scorn,
   The truth to her foreboding soul revealed;
Forth with her infant son she fled forlorn,
   And to his *Sire* above for aid appealed.

3 Her scanty bread and beverage are spent,
   Yet Ishmael sleeps unconscious of her pain;
A cry of agony to God is sent:
   "Would that the child would never wake again!"

4 The earth grows brighter where the mother stands,
   A hand divine arrests her falling tears;
A cloud of glory gilds the burning sands,
   And a celestial voice the mourner cheers.

5 "Arise and drink of yonder balmy well!
   Nor from the wilderness henceforward roam;
Father of nations *here* the lad shall dwell,
   With freedom blest for ages yet to come."

6 Oh, ever Bountiful! forsake us not,
   When driven forth to wander through life's waste;
But cheer with beams of love each barren spot,
   And let us of the spring of mercy taste.

P. M.

PSALM CXLV.

19 1 I will extol Thee, O my King!
   Thy holiness proclaim;
And earth with ev'ry voice shall sing,
   The glories of Thy name.

2 Thy tender mercies brightly shine,
    Immortal is Thy pow'r;
Thy *love* a beaming ray divine,
    That lights each passing hour.

3 The mem'ry of Thy goodness still
    Shall grateful hearts pervade;
Thy majesty and glory will
    For ever be displayed.

4 The eyes all shall wait on Thee,
    For perfect are Thy ways;
And pious hearts united be,
    O Maker! in Thy praise.   C. M. C.

8. DIVINE PROVIDENCE.

20   1 How cold that man! to faith how dead!
    Who, having nature's volume read,
      Finds not, from first to last,
    Some truth that to his moral sense
    Proves an eternal Providence—
      A present, future, past.

2 Below the brute *that* being ranks,
    Who fails to render grateful thanks,
      When he creation scans;
Where mountains lift their heads sublime,
    Gray witnesses from elder time,
      Of Wisdom's mighty plans.

3 Where forests wave and oceans flow,
    And light sheds an impartial glow,
      Like that of Mercy's rays;
Where gentle flowers yield their sweets,
    And ev'ry warbling bird repeats,
      Instinctive notes of praise.

4 Yet such there are in human kind,
　Whose souls to worldly claims resigned,
　　With apathy behold,
　Not only blossoms, hills and streams,
　But heaven with its starry beams
　　Of incorruptive gold.

5 Blind pilgrims these who grope their way,
　Without a guide their steps to sway,
　　Until a sudden fall
　Reminds them, when perhaps too late,
　Of those vicissitudes of fate
　　Which for religion call.

6 Oh! then will startled conscience seek
　Peace with an angry God to make,
　　And lips will move in prayer;
　Gracious and long-enduring Lord!
　Pardon e'en then wilt Thou accord,
　　If man but proves sincere.　　P. M.

Psalm LXXVII.

21

1 I will still remain with Thee,
　　My God! in each vicissitude;
　Though misfortune compass me,
　　My trust shall never be subdued.
　Father! to Thy hand I cling,
　Seeking refuge 'neath Thy wing.

2 When some bold inquirer asks:
　　Whom callest thou a gracious master?
　Is it love that overtasks?
　　Is it grace that brings disaster?
　Silencing the scoffer's strain,
　Faithful still do I remain.

3 Once again the scorner speaks :
   Why should the transgressor flourish?
Him who every statute breaks,
   Why should Heaven's bounty nourish?
Fool! the sun matures the seeds,
Both of flowers and of weeds.

4 But beyond life's little hour,
   Memory the blossom shieldeth ;
For each leaflet of the flower
   Still a grateful odor yieldeth ;
Whilst noxious plant, decayed,
Scentless in the dust is laid.

5 Thus embalmed, each spirit pure,
   By remembrance e'er is cherished ;
Where is then the evil doer?
   Where the place on which he perished?
Let oblivion answer this,
From its dark and dread abyss.

6 Lord! to Thee will I adhere,
   Though condemned in grief to languish;
Though the whole of my career
   May be spent in tears and anguish.
See I not a better land?
Hold I not a Father's hand?

7 Source of light and purity!
   Living, let truth my mind illume ;
God of all futurity!
   Unlock the portals of my tomb.
Let my *soul* the blessing gain,
With Thee ever to remain.   P. M.

22

1 We look to Thee, ineffable King!
    Whose spirit dust could organize,
Into each bright and beauteous thing,
    That in the globe's wide compass lies;
Paternal, providential Lord!
We look to Thee and praise accord.

2 We look to Thee, protective Power,
    Whose beauty for no claimant waits;
But freely flowing every hour,
    Thy children's wants anticipates.
To satisfy our soul's desire,
We look to Thee, almighty Sire!

3 We look to Thee when sorrow's season
    Covers with frost the head and heart;
When suffering from social treason,
    Friend after friend we see depart.
Thus desolate, O God! above,
We look to Thee alone for love.

4 We look to Thee when feeling gaineth
    Mastery o'er the moral sense;
When curb and counsel it disdaineth,
    By reason brought for its defence.
From this dread trial to be free,
Searcher of hearts! we look to Thee.

5 We look to Thee when we discover
    Death's shadow on our pathway rest;
When all life's interests are over,
    That once elated or depressed.
A better, brighter world to see,
Saviour and Lord! we look to Thee.

                                                           P. M.

9. DIVINE PROVIDENCE IN RELATION TO ISRAEL.

23
1 The sun shines on with glorious light,
   And smiles upon this world of ours;
The moon with lustre soft and bright,
   On earth her silver radiance pours.

2 'Tis God who wreathes the brow of night,
   With bands of burning, glitt'ring stars;
'Tis God, with endless power and might,
   Who moves the morning's golden bars.

3 And He, through all these works sublime,
   Looks down upon a favored race;
For Israel, from creation's time,
   Dwelt 'neath the wing of heavenly grace.

4 The light divine of holy love
   Still sheds on Judah's broken band
A halo beaming from above,
   And kindled by th' Almighty's hand.

C. M. C.

24
1 Lo! He sleeps and slumbers not,
   Israel's God and Guide!
Then, whatever be thy lot,
   In Him thy hope confide.
To Him be all thy heart resigned,
Whose hands alone its wounds can bind.
   Oh, fear not!
But trust to His paternal care,
All that on earth to thee is dear;
Never from remembrance blot:
Omnipotence slumbers not.

2 Lo! it sleeps and slumbers not,
    The providence of heaven!
But has watched o'er every spot,
    To which thou hast been driven.
Special hath been the protection
Of the race of its election.
    Tremble not!
But ever to his will conform,
Whose word can tranquilize the storm.
Who (oh! be it ne'er forgot,)
Ever present, slumbers not.

3 Lo! they sleep and slumber not,
    God's transcendent powers!
These all radiant beauties wrought,
    From stars, and gems, and flowers,
Brighter than all, man's spirit made,
In His similitude array'd.
    Despond not!
Love, that nature animated,
Will defend what it created;
Rock, worm, bud, in wisdom brought,
Say: God's power slumbers not!

4 Lo! it sleeps and slumbers not,
    That deep abiding love!
With forbearing patience fraught,
    That man's remorse should move.
That mightiest of attributes,
Which evil into good transmutes.
    Oh, weep not!
For in this charity divine,
Thou hast a token and a sign,
That whate'er God may allot,
His compassion slumbers not.

5 Lo! it sleeps and slumbers not,
    God's equity supreme!
That casts in every mortal's lot
    A shadow and a beam.
Whose bolt retributive descends
On him who 'gainst His law offends.
      Yet, doubt not
That he who acts a righteous part,
Will rest upon his Father's heart,
When that kingdom shall be sought,
Where pure justice slumbers not.

6 Lo! it sleeps and slumbers not,
    That all pervading grace,
That in palace and in cot,
    Leaves its benignant trace;
Whose radiations mild are thrown,
Unceasingly from zone to zone.
      Oh! linger not,
Thou wanderer from virtue's way,
To Providence contritely pray,
Mercy ne'er is vainly sought;
Judah's Guardian slumbers not.

P. M.

ISAIAH, CHAP. **XLIV.**

25 1 Fear not, fear not, O Jeshurun,
    My own, my chosen treasure!
Blessings are for thy offspring won,
    Yea, mercies without measure.

2 Like willows by the water-course,
    Ye righteous servants flourish;
My spirit, the unfailing source,
    That Jacob's seed shall nourish.

3 Idols of earth usurp my praise,—
    Beware, O cherished nation!
Lest ye your hearts in homage raise,
    To God's abomination.

4 "I am the first, I am the last;"
    Woe to the bold blasphemer!
Who shall some monstrous image cast,
    And call it his Redeemer.

5 Beneath the firmament's broad cope,
    Bear witness as ye gather,
That I *alone* am Israel's Hope,
    His Judge, his King, his Father.
                              P. M.

Psalm CXXVII.

26 1 Unless the land where ye abide,
    The care of Heaven boasts,
Falsely to watchmen ye confide
    The safety of its coasts.

2 Except the Lord will fortify
    The fabrics ye erect,
Vain are the pillars, strong and high,
    Of mortal architect.

3 Whether, O Judah! ye sojourn
    In deserts, towns, or tents,
To God, as to your fortress, turn
    Your tower of defence.

4 On land and sea, enslaved or free,
    His name alone extol;
Who is, who was, and e'er shall be,
    Guardian and King of all.   P. M.

III. MAN'S DIGNITY AND DESTINATION.

1. MAN'S DIGNITY.

27 1 O God! within Thy temple-walls,
　　Light my spirit seems, and free,
　Regardless of those worldly calls,
　　That withdraw it oft from Thee.
　Faith to the proudest whispers: Here
　　Riches are but righteous deeds,
　And he who dries a human tear,
　　Ne'er to mercy vainly pleads.

2 Can sorrow at Thy altar raise
　　The voice of lamentation?
　Oh, no! its plaint is changed to praise,
　　Regret, to Resignation.
　To naught all human evil shrinks,
　　Where revelation showeth
　That God each soul to heaven links,
　　Which ne'er in trust foregoeth.

3 Oh! Brightest, most benignant boon,
　　Above all others rated:
　With Thee, Creator to commune,
　　In temples consecrated;
　That when life's boundary is past,
　　More glorious still appears;
　Since sanctuary, we at last,
　　Find in celestial spheres,—

4 Where no distinction shall be found,
　　Between immortals heav'n born,
　And spirits that, by virtue crowned,
　　Once the chains of earth have worn.

Merciful Father! may Thy child
  Claim this privilege divine?
Shall I, by sinful thoughts defiled,
  Call a boon so precious mine?

5 My courage fails not, since Thy grace
    Exceeds in boundless measure,
  The guilt of that transgressive race
    Who kindle Thy displeasure.
  Therefore to the house of pray'r
    E'er will I my steps address,
  All Thy mercies to declare,
    While my errors I confess.   P. M.

2. MAN, THE IMAGE OF GOD.

28 1 Exult, my soul, in consciousness proud,
      That I in God's image was made:
    That 'mid nature's irrational crowd,
      Moral light to me was conveyed;
        When dust, by His pure breath refined,
        In flesh the "vital spark" enshrined.

  2 Oh! how shall I deserve the station
      Omnipotence assigns to me;
    Whose spiritual elevation
      Is next to angels in degree?
        How Mercy's likeness manifest,
        Reflected in each mortal breast?

  3 Perilous pre-eminence! to hold
      Perfection's model in the mind;
    Yet feel how the inferior mould
      In which its essence is confined,
        May all its majesty efface,
        And leave of stamp divine no trace.

4 Immortal reason! hast thou no beam
    Of bright intelligence to prove
Thy semblance to that Sire supreme,
    Whose breath is life, whose blessing love?
        Triumph! though passions dim thy ray,
        In thee God's image we survey.

5 Justice, by thee for e'er directed,
    His strongest feature typifies;
In truth (through reason best reflected)
    His spirit's light I recognise;
        And in beneficence e'er trace
        His brightest trait: celestial grace!

6 How glorious this filiation,
    Between the Lord of worlds and me!
Oh! how shall I deserve the station,
    Next to the angels in degree?
        Like these, by walking in His ways;
        Like these, by singing e'er His praise.

                      P. M.

3. VIRTUE.

29   1 God of power! in Thy gift
      Though countless blessings lie,
   My voice for *one alone* I lift,
      In prayer to Thee on high.

2 No covetous appeal for gold
    Shall from my lips proceed;
Nor by the love of fame controlled,
    For crowns of glory plead.

3 I ask but for the precious ore
    Contained in *Virtue's mine;*
And for her wreath that will endure,
    When diadems decline.

4 Of godliness, by Grace supreme,
   Would I become possessed;
Grant that its pure and perfect beam
   May on my spirit rest.

5 Let wisdom of the heart, O Lord!
   Be now and ever mine;
All else is but corruption's hoard,
   Dust, hiding light divine.   P. M.

30 1 Oh! what avails my destination,
   As immortality's great heir,
If I, regardless of salvation,
   Do not my soul for this prepare?
If to the world's illusive pleasures
   My spirit hourly I yield,
And for its frail and fleeting treasures,
   Uncultured leave fair virtue's field?

2 And what is temporal ambition,
   That never yet fruition found?
A most unhallowed superstition
   In deities, *itself* hath crowned.
That in its soul false idols setting,
   Makes their decree a law supreme,—
The statutes of *that* God forgetting,
   Whose power can alone redeem.

3 Mean avarice! how low the perches
   To which *thy* grasping talons cling;
Thy downward glance unwearied searches
   For gold,—thy precious phantom-king.
Barren the ground in which it lieth,
   Buried and hidden from thy view;
And nature to its grave denieth
   Flowers, she elsewhere loves to strew.

4 Should I *not* yield to the temptations
   Of passions fierce and wild as these,
Self-worship still exacts oblations
   That will not less my God displease—
To my *own* service consecrating
   All that *His* bounteous hand conferred;
My neighbor ne'er conciliating,
   By gift of love or gentle word.

5 Gracious Creator! ere I perish,
   Let me my trespasses retrieve;
Righteous desires let me cherish,
   And works of godliness achieve.
In Thy covenant let me rejoice,
   And in its precepts persevere,
For life's chief ornament, making choice
   Of Truth, whose crown the angels wear.

6 When in the valley of death I walk,
   Firm be my step, my mind serene;
There, on my God, Redeemer and Rock,
   Will I in trust unfalt'ring lean.
My soul shall not tremble while waiting
   Its sentence within the dark tomb;
But heaven *beyond* contemplating,
   Shrink not from its prelusive gloom.

                                P. M.

4. PIETY.

31 1 Oh! turn at meek devotion's call
   From idle dreams of worldly power;
Which flourishes awhile, to fall
   And perish, like an earth-born flower.

2 Countless are pleasure's bright decoys,
   Unwary mortals to ensnare;

Faith beckons thee from barren joys,
   And points to her immortal sphere.

3 Wouldst thou thy soul to God commend?
   Forsake the scene of heartless mirth;
Seek those who weep without a friend,
   Bring wine and oil to suff'ring worth.

4 Let piety direct thy choice,
   In all thy spirit's high concerns;
Then shall the pilgrim's heart rejoice,
   Who in the "vale of tears" sojourns.
                                 P. M.

32
1 How long will man in pleasure merged,
   Religion's claims neglect?
How long, by worldly interest urged,
   Her warning hints reject?

2 Vain prodigal of precious time!
   Were mental gifts bestowed
To waste in folly or in crime,
   Oblivious of thy God?

3 When surfeited with life's repast,
   Its sweetness turned to gall,
Thy conscience will be roused at last,
   And death thy soul appal.

4 Will worshipers of gold then fly,
   Thy dying couch to cheer?
Thy *spirit's* cravings to supply,
   Will Mirth desert her sphere?

5 No! Piety forsaken long,
   Invoked with earnest zeal,
Will, even *then*, forget her wrong,
   And answer thy appeal.

6 But better, wiser far are all,
    Whose youth devoutly past,
On heaven's "Great Physician" call
    With confidence at last.   P. M.

33 1 Man of the world! wilt thou not pause,
And give thy heart to Heaven's cause?
In paths of interest wilt thou plod,
Forgetful of the Lord thy God?

2 Oh! turn away from life's parade,
Before thy soul hath been betrayed
From virtue's eminence to stoop,
And forfeit its eternal hope.

3 What purer pleasures wouldst thou taste,
Than are by piety embraced?
What higher prize couldst thou obtain,
Than thy Creator's love to gain?

4 The wealth and glory of the skies
Are won, by generous sacrifice,
By him who selfish joy foregoes
To mitigate another's woes;

5 Whose resignation, calm and meek,
Will humbly of God's chastening speak:
Whose soul from perjury is free,
And worships but *one* Deity.

6 Man of the world! no gift of thine
Compares with Mercy's pledge divine,
Which pardon to each sinner yields,
Whose spirit true contrition feels.   P. M

34 1 In holiness, Eternal Lord!
    Thy servant would excel:

Oh! let its spirit in each word
   And in each action dwell.

2 No strength have I to combat long
   With passions fierce and wild;
Nor hope amid corruption's throng,
   To wander undefiled.

3 For self-direction too unwise,
   For self-defence too frail;
On godliness my hope relies,
   Their spells to countervail.

4 This shall my heart's best warder prove,
   When proud and venal foes
Presume against benignant love,
   Its avenues to close.

5 This shall from avarice secure
   Thy worshiper's weak thought,
By showing that its golden lure,
   True bliss hath never caught.

6 From envy, vanity, and pride,
   This, too, my soul shall save;
O gracious God! O holy Guide!
   Grant me the grace I crave.   P. M.

35 1 "Blest is the man to whom the Lord
   No iniquity e'er imputes,"
Who hath the grounds of truth explored,
   And meekly gleaned its godly fruits.

2 Above all mortals, blest is he
   Who, from temptation's tangled maze,
Hath set his struggling spirit free
   To walk in God's appointed ways.

3 King of the universe! impart
    To me that energy divine,
  Which nerves the weak and wayward heart,
    Unrighteous feelings to resign.

4 With Thine immortal presence fill
    The depths of my degenerate soul;
  Subject its motions to Thy will,
    Its passions to Thy pure control.

5 Oh! let Thine interdict suffice
    Each wrong desire to restrain;
  From what a Father's law denies,
    Let me in filial love refrain.

6 Care shall not enter then my breast,
    Now to solicitude a prey;
  No bitter thought shall break my rest,
    No danger then my sense dismay.

7 Welcome the moment that shall bring
    A boon so earnestly desired!
  And which from Thee alone must spring,
    From whom all blessings are acquired.

P. M.

36 1 Oh! how imperfect, blind, and false,
       Does *that* faith to me appear,
     Which from all moral law revolts,
       And exhausts itself in prayer:
     That more its sanctity displays
     In holy words than holy ways.

2 Know we not, from revelation,
    What true piety dictates?
  Is not *Love* the best oblation
    That its altar decorates?

The love that with our neighbor shares,
   In brotherhood, life's joys and cares?

3 Benevolence, whose varied alms,
      Dealt alike by heart and hand,
   Now virtue's wounded spirit calms,
      Now relieves want's famished band,—
   Making an Eden oft to bloom,
   E'en amid desolation's gloom.

4 *Trust*, that firmly stands its trial
      With the arrow in its breast;
   Meek *forgiveness, self-denial*,
      These are Faith's sublimest test
   Worship like this will supersede
   The *lip's* loud echo of her creed.

5 Oh! wherefore *Heaven's will* rehearse
      In a grave and measured tone,
   If the ungodly and perverse
      To *that* will prefer their own?
   And deem their sacred duties o'er
   When they in prayer their feelings pour?

6 Though precepts may be multiplied,
      Mercy's aim is not fulfilled;
   Earth must by us be beautified,
      Truth alone its shrines must build,—
   Uprooting thence corruption's weeds,
   To plant religion's purest seeds. P. M.

37 1 The heavens, Almighty! Thy glory declare,
         The earth with Thy riches abounds;
      Thy provident presence is felt everywhere,
         Thy name through all nature resounds.

2 Day showeth to day the pavilion of light
   In which Thou hast made Thine abode;
   And night, breaking silence, extolleth to night
   The knowledge and power of God.

3 Thou canst not, O man! 'neath the firmament stand
   With the fixed star of faith in thy breast,
   Not lifting in homage thy heart and thy hand,
   His wisdom and truth to attest.

4 Yet think not in verbal devotion alone,
   Thou hast all thy duty achieved;
   For prayer without *practice* ne'er reaches the throne
   From whence all thy gifts are received.

5 Thou canst not declare that the way is unknown,
   In which thou'rt required to walk;
   For never had pilgrim as true a guide-stone
   As the tablet on Horeb's high rock.

6 Though feeble thy step, if thy *purpose* be strong,
   Life's journey directed by this,
   Shall close without fear that the mem'ry of wrong
   Will cloud the soul's prospect of bliss.

                                          P. M.

38 1 Lord, my Redeemer and my Rock!
        Grant me Thy aid divine
     To keep Thy judgments, and to walk
        In truth's unerring line.

2 Thou, who hast charge of human kind,
    Thy suppliant e'er save
From all that vitiates the mind,
    Or may the heart deprave.

3 An infant's helplessness is mine,
    When strong temptations rise,
And bid me heaven's hope resign
    For some unhallowed prize.

4 Perhaps a plume from glory's wing,
    A link from pleasure's chain,
A harp without *one* holy string,
    For pure devotion's strain.

5 Alas! how poor is either meed
    For an immortal soul;
Yet oft for these will it recede
    From its celestial goal.

6 God of compassion! to Thy care
    My spirit I commend;
Let it to Thee unblemished bear
    The likeness Thou didst lend.   P. M.

5. IMMORTALITY OF THE SOUL.

39 1 God of my fathers! merciful and just,
Who into being shaped this breathing dust,
Teach me its rebel passions to control,—
Pour Thy influence o'er my restless soul.

2 Teach me to look beyond the gloomy grave;
For Thou, O Father! still art nigh to save,
When rising from the dark and cheerless tomb,
I'll walk with Thee in renovated bloom.

3 E'en at Thine altar as I bend the knee,
   My heart expands, my hopes increase in Thee;
Aspiring man forgets that he is earth,
And clings to Thee for an immortal birth.
                            C. D. L. H.

40 1 When morning paints the eastern sky
   In rich and varied hues of light,
Before Thy Throne, O Lord! most high,
Let *all* confess Thy pow'r and might.

2 When twilight's shadows gently fall,
   When evening's thousand stars appear,
When midnight's gloom o'ershadows all,
   We'll think of Thee with hope and fear.

3 We seek Thee in the hour of joy,
   In sorrow bow before Thy will;
Thou canst life's feeble chords destroy,
   In death each pulse for ever still.

4 But Thou wilt still preserve the *soul*,
   When purified from earthly stain,
When soaring to that heavenly goal,
   It seeks immortal life to gain.   C. M. C.

41 1 A mournful lament for the dead!
   Woe unto me! it is gone;
The delight of my heart is fled;
   My joy from earth is withdrawn.

2 Whither shall I, broken-hearted,
   Find balsam for wounds so deep?
Silent remain the departed,
   My tears disturb not their sleep.

3 Thus e'er when the last angel calls,
    Man waileth around the tomb;
Thus ever when life's blossom falls,
    Surrenders his soul to gloom.

4 Oh! would he turn *upward* the eye
    Despair has fixed in the dust,
A voice would from thence fortify
    His faith, his hope, and his trust.

5 Immoderate grief is unbelief;
    Hear Omnipotence and heed!
If immortality's first leaf
    Spring from Corruption's seed,

6 Why then in horror e'er recoil
    From the mention of decay,
That hath no power to despoil
    Aught beyond the breathing clay?

7 Think not my providence will cease
    O'er my children in the grave;
Death, my messenger of peace,
    Frees the soul my grace will save.

8 Thy God, thy Father, this proclaims,
    Whose promise will ne'er deceive.
Then tremble not at empty names,
    Ye who Mercy's word believe.   P. M.

42 1 Though man of all the ruin hears
    By time or tempest wrought;
One ray throughout all gloom appears
    By hope from heaven brought.

2 For though the mighty waters shrink
    From oceans into rills,

And nature's lofty bulwarks sink
  From mountains into hills;

3 Though these, with many frailer things,
    Perish and pass away;
  Faith to the holy promise clings,
    That triumphs o'er decay.

4 Man's spirit, by divine decree,
    The stroke of death defies;
  And from the bonds of death set free,
    Immortal shall arise.   P. M.

43 1 Through the valley of tears as we thought-
      fully stray,
    Where the wrecks of mortality lie;
  Let the spirit of faith spring from dust and
      decay
    To Omnipotence throned in the sky.

2 The date of a star, (that bright firmament
      flower,)
    Is as brief in eternity's sphere,
  As the blossom that breathes out its life in
      an hour,
    Nevermore upon earth to appear.

3 With that region of infinite Glory compared,
    Where ages like moments take flight,
  The world seems a cell for man's dwelling
      prepared,
    Till his soul grows familiar with light.

4 Yea, the earth is a place of probation and
      pray'r,
    Wherein beggars for bounty divine,

  Still their sorrows and wounds, to their
   Father declare,
 That His hand to relief may incline.

5 But in heaven the voice of petition shall
  cease,
 And loud praises for ever resound
To the merciful God, for the spirit's release
 From the shackles by which it was bound.
        P. M.

6. COMMEMORATION OF THE DEAD.

Part First.

44 1 O man! frail child of finite pow'rs!
  Nature, by changeless order,
 Places thy cradle 'mid the flow'rs
  That on the grave-yard border.
   Though youth, while at play
   In life's vernal ray,
  Will not take for death's token
  Blossoms withered and broken.

2 And truth from age to age repeats
  At every pilgrim's portal:
 Life as a shadow from thee fleets,
  Remember, thou art mortal;
 Wake at that call, wild dreamer!
  And, by its warning guided,
 Be yet the wise redeemer
  Of time to thee confided.
 Woe! fragile being of an hour,
  Prey to annihilation's power.

3 But wherefore, man, in thy serenest mood,
 When joy upon thee flashes,
 Still minglest thou with songs of gratitude
  Sad thoughts of dust and ashes?
 Wilt thou no hint from frailer natures take?
  From flowers, that at eve appear to die,
 Yet 'neath the canopy of heaven wake
  To greet God's morning messenger on high?

Part Second.

45 1 O Thou! who dwell'st in heights supernal,
 God! self-existent and eternal!
 What traveler shall reach Thy mountain?
 What thirsting spirit taste Thy fountain?

2 Mortal! in thee resides the power,
 Of gaining access unto each;
 But he who would to heaven tower,
  Must first the height of virtue reach;
 Must see in holiness a beauty
  Earth rivals not in all its bound;
 Ne'er mock at truth, nor turn from duty
  Idly to tread life's pleasure ground.
 Then shall the recording angel render
  Account of all thy righteous ways,
 And crowning thee, reveal the splendor
  Thy Father's blessed realm displays.

3 Woe! woe! to the immortal soul
 That virtue's voice ne'er heeds,
 When justice reads the roll
  Of its ungodly deeds.

4 Joy to the pure and pious breast
 That darkness never heedeth ;
With light from spheres celestial blest,
 When life's last sun recedeth.

5 The soul religion trained from youth
 To scorn the world's dominion,
Shall reach the native land of truth
 With free and fearless pinion.

6 Triumph ? ye but escape a prison,
 When death the vital chord doth sever ;
Triumph ! when mercy's star hath risen
 To guide ye to your God for ever.
Triumph ! on eagle's wings ye tower
 Up to eternity's bright portals ;
Triumph ! time hastens to the hour
 That gives ye place with the immortals.

IV. RELATION BETWEEN GOD AND MAN.

1. REVELATION.

46
1 Let choral songs of gladness flow,
 The Lord of hosts to praise ;
Who deigned on darkened minds to throw
 The law's enlight'ning rays.

2 No plea hath Israel for crime ;
 Since God's paternal grace
To him revealed those truths sublime,
 Which time can ne'er efface.

3 Before our eyes then let us set
 Our Father's bond of love ;

With praise repay our filial debt
    To Him who reigns above.

4 Let Sinai proudly lift her head
    Above the hills of earth:
For God thereon His glory shed
    At revelation's birth

5 Exalt the Lord! to whom we owe
    The first and latter rain,
And dews from Mercy's fount that flow
    To bless the thirsty plain.

6 As those refreshing showers tend
    To fertilize the field;
Thy laws, O God! our hearts amend,
    And virtue's harvest yield.   P. M

2. DIVINE LAW.

47 1 Lord! when I hear Thy holy law,
    Its spirit let me comprehend,
And meditate with silent awe
    On words that to salvation tend.

2 Oh! far above the finest gold
    Thy testimonies I esteem;
These shall my faltering feet uphold,
    My steps from evil paths redeem.

3 To Thee will I my prayers address,
    The free-will offerings of my soul;
Guardian! through life's dark wilderness,
    Do Thou my erring course control.

4 Oh! let unblemished truth alone
    My heart and mind for e'er inspire;

That I may, in its purest tone,
   Extol my gracious King and Sire. P. M.

3. RELIGION.

48 1 To smile when we on life's breakers are tost,
      And serenely its tempest survey ;
   To say, though the beacon of hope is lost,
      Mercy's star will direct our way :
         Such trust in trial's hour
         Springs from religion's pow'r.

2 At morn, with cheerful emotions to rise,
      Glorifying the Giver of rest ;
   Ne'er to let sleep our senses surprise,
      Ere the world's Benefactor is blest :
         Such is the righteous course
         Man's reason should enforce.

3 With high resolve in duty's path to tread,
      Though it may our fondest wish frustrate ;
   Nor ever by temptation to be led,
      Virtue's sacred laws to violate :
         Faith only nerves the soul
         To this great self-control.

4 To live in harmony with all mankind,
      Injuries with favors to requite ;
   To hold God's image in the heart enshrined,
      Nor by sin its purity to blight :
         This shall our peace insure,
         Now, and for evermore.

5 Undazzled by gold, by menace unmoved,
      One sole Being Supreme to cherish ;
   To be firm in the faith our fathers loved,
      Though for this as martyrs we perish :

>   To piety alone
>   Such fortitude is known.
>
> 6 To make decay familiar to the mind,
>   And in death God's messenger perceive,
>   Who, when the mortal breath has been resigned,
>   Will the soul to its Redeemer leave:
>   What but religion can
>   Reveal this gracious plan?   P. M.

49 1 Remember, man! while thou art young,
     To turn thy heart towards the Lord,
   Ere sorrow hath thy bosom wrung,
     Or life hath "loosed its silver chord."

2 Spring hath its flowers,—youth its sweets,
    Cradled in both the canker lies;
  And when *one little* season fleets,
    Man's spirit droops—the blossom dies.

3 Ye triflers on the brink of time,
    Scorn not the sage and silver-haired,
  When they forewarn ye in your prime
    To be for evil days prepared.

4 Strong as ye are, shall ye not fall
    Down to the dust at God's decree?
  Proud as ye are, shall not the pall
    Mantle your frail mortality?

5 Praise the Creator, ere decay
    Your energies shall paralyze,
  Or darkness, in the latter day,
    Shall hide the heavens from your eyes.
                                        P. M.

50 1 Blest are the enlight'ners of mankind,
　　Thrice blest the holy teacher,
Who, with a pure and patient mind,
　　Instructs his fellow-creature,—
Who, swayed by virtue's golden rule,
　　Would her precepts inculcate,
And in her chaste and godly school,
　　Erring spirits educate.

2 All are Thy ministers, O Lord!
　　Who, imprest with truth divine,
Speed the work, and speak the word
　　That shall make its light to shine,—
Who in flowers that blush below,
　　And in stars that beam above,
A glory and perfection show,
　　That to faith the heart must move.

3 All who, uprooting error's weeds,
　　Leave for moral culture room,
And with imperishable seeds,
　　Cause the barren mind to bloom,—
Interpreters of Heaven's law,
　　May its God their efforts guide,
And to celestial regions draw
　　Souls who thus have lived and died.

　　　　　　　　　　　　P. M.

Psalm CXLIV.

51 1 Lord! what is man, that Thou should'st take
　　Account or knowledge of his ways?
Like shadows from the summer lake,
　　Briefly depart his measured days.

2 Yet, though but vanity and dust,
　　Oh! hear Thy worshiper sincere,

Who now appeals with humble trust,
    That Thou wilt grant his earnest prayer.

3 Through the world may Israel's youth,
    Like branches of some goodly tree,
Enlightened by the rays of truth,
    Flourish in grace and dignity.

4 Dispersed in many climes and zones,
    May Judah's sprightly daughters be
Polished, as are the corner-stones
    In palaces of royalty.

5 May these, above all earthly fame,
    The favor of their God esteem,
And merit that distinguished name,
    The chosen race of the Supreme.   P. M.

4. DUTIES TOWARDS GOD.

1. ACQUISITION OF THE KNOWLEDGE OF THE LORD.

52 1 Glory not in a gift so vain
    As worldly knowledge, ye discreet!
Whose stream, like the treacherous main,
    Rolls onward awhile to retreat.
But wisdom by faith purified
    Is light radiating afar,
And love for your heavenly Guide
    Its brightest and loveliest star.

2 Glory not, O ye that are strong!
    For on dust your vigor is based;
Strength only to him can belong
    Whose spirit by virtue is braced,

'Gainst passions that nature disturb,
  This, this is man's moral resource;
No power their progress to curb
  Resides in corporeal force.

3 Glory not! ye rich in your gold!
  More brittle is this than the reed;
Beware! lest its glittering mould
  The pathway to heaven impede.
True honor it can ne'er impart,
  Nor solace in sorrow afford;
Rather pray for a guileless heart,
  That trustingly turns to its Lord.

4 Glory in wisdom that augments
  Your knowledge of a God supreme,
Who will, as virtue's recompense,
  Man's spirit from the grave redeem.
Glory in energy of soul,
  That truth's assailants will oppose,
And with a mighty self-control,
  Crush all religion's bosom foes.

5 There is a wealth of words in prayer,
  Though poor the suppliant may be,
And themes for many volumes rare,
  In every work of God ye see.
Yours be the gold that never frets,
  The wisdom-star that never wanes;
The honor that remembers debts
  Due to the Source of all your gains.

                                P. M.

2. OBEDIENCE TO THE WILL OF GOD.

Genesis, Chap. I.

53
1 Formless and void creation stood,
    The deep in darkness lay;
  When from Thy spirit, Lord! the flood
    Borrowed a quick'ning ray.

2 Light from the gates of heaven beamed
    On flower, herb, and fruit;
  Each element with tenants teemed,
    Fish, reptile, bird, and brute.

3 A glowing firmament was seen
    The waters to divide,
  Whose lustrous orbs seemed links between
    Earth's pilgrim and his Guide.

4 A thousand witnesses appeared,
    God's love to testify;
  Mountains and hills His might declared,
    And bowed as He passed by.

5 Man by the tree of knowledge stood,
    Master of all around;
  And woman, in her softest mood,
    The gifts of mercy crowned.

6 They sin, they fall,—oh! weep and pray,
    That, tempted, ye may turn
  From all forbidden things away,
    Nor God's displeasure earn

7 By doubts of His almighty word
    Or His all-perfect ways;
  But, firm in faith, obey the Lord,
    And all His judgments praise.   P. M.

JOB, CHAP. IX.

54
1 Oh! how shall man with God contend,
    Mighty in strength and wise of heart?
Or hope to prosper in his end,
    Who blindly plays so bold a part?

2 Frail, finite mortal! shall I stand
    In judgment with the King of kings.
Who can the rising sun command
    To gather up His golden wings:

3 Conceal his light, his course arrest;
    Seal up the stars; the heavens spread;
Move mountains from their place of rest:
    And on the waves of ocean tread?

4 Should I my righteousness rehearse,
    Or boast my constant rectitude?
What perfect seemed, might prove perverse,
    When by the eye of Heaven viewed.

5 I will not reason or reply,
    But supplicate the Judge Supreme,
My soul with hope to fortify,
    That I may bless His holy name.   P. M.

55
1 Though sorrows may be multiplied,
    And cares around thee throng,
In Israel's Guardian still confide,
    And lift thy voice in song.

2 Wilt thou on gold or glory dote,
    Or covet pomp and power?
Bubbles that on life's current float,
    To break in one brief hour?

3 Though health and competence be thine,
   And peace thy portion crown,
Will thine ungrateful spirit pine
   To reach at high renown?

4 As well might stars rebellious turn
   From their allotted spheres,
Ambitious of the solar urn,
   More bright and vast than theirs.

5 Oh! not to *question* but *obey*
   The great Creator's word,
Was intellect's transcendent ray
   On human dust conferred.

6 *Praise* is the noble privilege
   On man alone bestowed;
Redeem, immortal soul, thy pledge,
   Extol the living God.   P. M.

GENESIS, CHAP. XXVII.

56 1 Deep silence reigned in Isaac's tent,
   His voice was faint, his vigor spent,
Dim were his eyes, for death was near,
   He spoke, and Esau bowed to hear:

2 Away, my first-born, to the field!
   Thy quiver take, thy weapons wield;
And let thy filial hand supply
   Sweet nutriment before I die.

3 That life to God I'll soon resign,
   Once ransomed from Moriah's shrine;
Blest shalt thou be, e'er I depart.
   Child of my heritage and heart.

4 Cheered is the dying patriarch,
　But age hath made his sense too dark
　To heed the bold supplanter's lure,
　His primal blessing to secure.

5 Earth's fatness and the dews of heav'n,
　To thee, young Israel! are given;
　No portion can the prophet's word
　To Edom promise, but the sword.

6 Too late he mourns his lost birthright,
　Contemned through carnal appetite;
　Omnipotence decrees this fate,
　His outraged laws to vindicate.

7 Such is the lot the frail deserve,
　Who unto idol worship swerve,
　The favor of some heart to win,
　Sunk like itself in mortal sin.

8 Strengthen me, Lord! with moral power
　Safely to pass temptation's hour;
　Nor let me ever lightly prize
・Aught that Thy wisdom sanctifies.　　P. M.

3. FAITH IN GOD.

57 1 I weep not now as once I wept,
　　　At fortune's strokes severe;
　　Since faith hath to my bosom crept,
　　　And placed a buckler there.

2 Lightly upon this holy shield
　　Falls sorrow's thorny rod,
　And he who wears it learns to yield
　　Submissively to God.

3 It breaks the force of ev'ry dart
   By disappointment hurled
Against the shrinking human heart,
   In this cold, callous world.

4 Wrestling with this, I have defied
   All that my peace assailed;
Passion subdued hath turned aside,
   And sin before it quailed.

5 How many wounds would now be mine,
   How many pangs intense!
But for the shield of faith divine,
   My spirit's strong defence.

6 Oh! when in prayer my hands I lift
   To Thee, Almighty God!
The excellence of this Thy gift,
   With fervor will I laud.   P. M.

58 1 O God! to Thy paternal grace,
   That ne'er its bounty measures,
All gifts Thy grateful children trace,
   That constitutes life's pleasures.

2 Light, being, liberty, and joy,
   All, all to Thee are owing;
Nor can another hand destroy
   Blessings of Thy bestowing.

3 None, save our own; for in man's heart
   Such passions are secreted,
That peace affrighted weeps apart,
   To see Thy aim defeated.

4 *Light* is made dim by human guile,
   Existence doth but languish.

  And *freedom* loses her bright smile
   'Mid scenes of strife and anguish.

5 Father! though forfeited by sin
 Are all Thy tender mercies;
There is a *trusting faith* within
 That ev'ry fear disperses.

6 Honor and praise to Thee belong,
 O God of our salvation!
Who will defend from shame and wrong
 Thy first elected nation.

7 Protector of the quick and dead!
 Thy love *this* **world** o'erfloweth;
And, when the "vital spark" hath fled,
 Eternal life bestoweth.   P. M.

Psalm XXXVII.

59 1 Let thy heart forever delight in the Lord,
  Though its purity malice assaileth;
For naught that detractors may breathe or record
  Against innocence ever prevaileth.

2 The slanderer's shaft on himself shall recoil,
  By the heavenly Father reverted;
Whose hand cutteth down the green herb to the soil,
  And the being that justice perverted.

3 Fret not thyself when prosperity bringeth
  Treasures untold to the proud and unjust;
Righteousness over their sepulchres singeth:
  "Gold cannot ransom the soul from the dust."

4 From evil depart; let wrath be forsaken;
  Meekness and truth God's blessings
      shall merit,
    Let poverty's plaint thy pity awaken,
      Thou, who the gifts of earth wouldst
          inherit.

5 Awhile the transgressor may seem to tower
    Like a green bay-tree in the genial ray;
  But his seed shall perish in life's first hour,
    And his land to strangers shall pass
        away.

6 Oh! follow the perfect man—mark the
        upright,
    For to him salvation and peace belong;
  His judgments are clear as meridian light,
    And the branch of his root shall flourish
        long.   P. M.

Psalm XXXVIII.

60 1 Rebuke me not nor chasten me,
      In Thy displeasure, Lord!
    But let a frail transgressor be
      To virtue's path restored.

2 My heart like grass is withered up,
    Sorrow my strength destroys;
  Sin's bitter drop within my cup,
    Life's sparkling draught alloys.

3 In vain my spirit seeks repose
    From all its worldly cares;
  Mine adversaries round me close,
    They compass me with snares.

4 My friends and kinsmen stand aloof,
    And mock me from afar;
  My soul, untouched by their reproof,
    Turns to its guiding **Star**.

5 For with unbroken trust will I
    In Thee, my God! confide,
  Who deigns the meek to dignify,
    The arrogant to chide.   P. M.

4. HOPE IN GOD.

Psalm CXXI.

61
1 I lift mine eyes unto the hills,
    And to the boundless sky,
  Thro' all life's sad and varied ills,
    Our help is from on high.

2 The heavenly King, who e'er shall be,
    In might eternal reigns;
  When sorrow's darts encompass me,
    He every hope sustains.

3 The burning rays of noon-tide sun,
    Shall smite me not by day;
  And while the evil path I shun,
    God will protect my way.

4 On every side *He* is my shade,
    And still preserves my soul;
  His greatness ever is displayed
    Thro' years that onward roll.

5 From this time, and for evermore,
    His mercy mildly beams;
  Lord! lead me to that heavenly shore,
    Where peace eternal gleams.   C. M. C.

62 1 Though I from kindred meet but scorn,
And am by parents left forlorn:
Still my heart, absolved from wrong,
Lifts to God its grateful song.

2 Thy countenance, celestial Sire!
With courage shall my soul inspire,
Meekly man's contempt to bear,
And all worldly woe and care.

3 Mark *him** from whom all Israel sprang;
Keenly he feels the parting pang,
When from kindred far removed,
And from childhood's home beloved.

4 Then was the angel's ladder brought
Before the dreaming exile's thought,
Which the righteous soul might teach
How the throne of God to reach.

5 From base to summit, the blest youth
Beheld progressive steps to truth,
Beaming with immortal bands
That reveal their Maker's plans.

6 These to the sleeper heaven ope,
Whence issue thrilling words of hope:
"Son of man! I am with thee
Wheresoever thou mayst flee."

7 And is not God's paternal tone
To Jacob's chosen offspring known?
Is there no celestial gate
To the *House* we consecrate?

* Genesis, chap. xxvii. 10, 17.

8 Devotion *here* a ladder rears,
  Whose golden steps are guileless prayers;
  These will the angel-forms disclose,
  When the soul here seeks repose.

9 Therefore in filial trust will I
  To Thee, my God, in sorrow fly:
  If, though wounded and forlorn,
  In my heart guilt hides no thorn.   P. M.

PSALM XLII. v. 11.

63 1 "Why art thou cast down, my soul?"
   Does not a God in heaven reign,
  And each human lot control,
   Whether with pleasure fraught or pain?
  Will He not life's bark conduct,
   Tho' darkness hides the treach'rous shoal
  That thy passage would obstruct?
   "Why art thou cast down, my soul?"

2 "Why art thou disquieted?"
   Terror *his* bosom agitates
  Who in sin has rioted,
   And Heaven's wrath anticipates;
  But he whose breast is free from guilt,
   Undaunted hears His thunders roll,
  His trust on grace divine is built;
   What disquiets thee, my soul?

3 "Oh! forever hope in God!"
   Who has countless suns created,
  And enamelled earth's green sod
   By their beams illuminated:—
  Who from ruin joy can bring
   To the believer's blest abode,

And make the mourner's heart to sing:
  "Oh! forever hope in God."

4 "Thou shalt praise and thank Him yet!"
    Joyfully to *Him* confessing,
  Thou in *seeming* blight hast met
    Oft a parent's *real* blessing,—
  Him who, on the grave's dark brink,
    Has salvation's fountain set,
  That each godly soul may drink:
    "Thou shalt praise and thank *Him* yet."

5 "My support and help art Thou,"
    Lord! when clouds of sadness lower,
  Rock of my defence art Thou,
    O gracious God! in peril's hour.
  Star to star and deep to deep
    Thy providence do e'er avow:
  My song with theirs shall concert keep;
    "My support and help art Thou."

P. M.

64 1 When grief on the heart has weighed
    Till its finest chords are hushed,
  And feelings that hope once swayed,
    By clamorous cares are crushed:
  Remember, God most prizes
  Those whom His rod chastises.

  2 When man no respite taketh
    From trouble, pain, or sorrow,
  But from brief slumber waketh
    To toils and cares each morrow:
  To God if he still turneth,
  His trust God's blessing earneth.

3 When, by the world neglected,
   Alone thou bravest dangers;
When those thy heart selected,
   From friends are changed to strangers:
Look! lorn pilgrim, look above
For better life and stronger love.

4 And oh! when death advances,
   Tremble not at the vision,
But meet with smiling glances,
   That *angel of transition*,
Whose scythe the fetter cleaveth,
That thy bruised spirit grieveth.   P. M.

5. LOVE OF GOD.

65

1 Oh! love the Lord with all thy *heart;*
   Its best affections sacrifice,
Rather than from *His* law depart,
   Who is most holy, just, and wise.

2 Oh! love the Lord with all thy *soul,*
   Which bears a principle divine,
That shall beyond its human goal
   Among angelic natures shine.

3 Oh! love the Lord with all thy *might;*
   For He has made thy spirit strong,
Firmly to wrestle for the right,
   And fearlessly resist the wrong.

4 Oh! love the Lord! to *Him* devote
   Thy time, thy treasure, and thy thought;
Let these each holy scheme promote,
   By which salvation may be wrought.

5 Oh! love the Lord! who, from thy birth
   To life's last moment, naught denies,
And after death commands the earth
   To yield the spirit to the skies.   P. M.

6. GRATITUDE TOWARDS GOD.

66 1 With ardent love and reverence deep,
   We bow before Thee, gracious Lord;
Whose marvels we in memory keep,
   Whose mercies on our hearts record;
And with a fervent gratitude,
Praise Thee for gifts each day renewed.

2 For that *first* life, from dust created,
   Which, though fragile as the flowers,
By Thine own image animated,
   O'er the dust in triumph towers:
For bounties every day renewed,
Father! accept our gratitude.

3 For verdant earth for ever teeming
   With beautiful and balmy forms;
For light, from star and planet streaming,
   Whose glow all nature cheers and warms:
For blessings every day renewed,
Father! accept our gratitude.

4 For memory's amazing powers.
   Long buried treasures to restore,
And make felicity's dead flowers
   Bloom in her atmosphere once more:
For blessings every day renewed,
Father! accept our gratitude.

5 For *conscience*, every thought arresting,
   Its purity to scrutinize;

  By virtue's moral standard testing
   The good or ill that in it lies:
  For bounties every day renewed,
  Father! accept our gratitude.

6 But chiefly for that love paternal
   Which for Thy children hath ordained
  A *second* life in realms eternal,
   If faith on earth their souls sustained:
  For an existence thus renewed,
  O God! accept our gratitude.   P. M.

67 1 To man with reason's gift endued,
   The pleasing task pertains,
  Of pouring forth his gratitude
   In pure and pious strains.

2 Lo! how the branches of a tree
   Back to its root convey
  The sap that gave vitality
   To blossom, fruit, and spray.

3 From mute, external nature, then,
   A gentle lesson learn;
  With filial love, ye sons of men,
   Parental care return.

4 Let gratitude within each breast
   Exert its high control;
  Its presence, like an angel guest,
   Shall sanctify the soul.

5 Canst thou, O Jeshurun! forget
   Thy Benefactor's claim?
  The God who o'er all others set
   Thy nation, faith and name?

6 Oh! let us in His praise unite,
    Who gave with liberal hand
Life, liberty, and moral light,
    His law to understand.   P. M.

7. SUBMISSION TO THE WILL OF GOD.

68
1 God Supreme! to Thee I pray,
Let my lips be taught to say,
Whether good or ill may flow,
Hallelujah, be it so!

2 What Thy wisdom may dictate
Let Thy servant vindicate,
Though it may my hopes o'erthrow,
Hallelujah, be it so!

3 Friends may falsify my trust,
Kindred also prove unjust,
Wound my heart and chill its glow,—
Hallelujah, be it so!

4 Health and comfort may decline,
Why at this should I repine?
Both to Thee, my God, I owe,
Hallelujah, be it so!

5 When by disappointment stung,
Hard it is for human tongue
Still to say, though tears may flow,
Hallelujah, be it so!

6 Yet, from Mercy's aid shall spring
Strength of spirit still to sing
'Mid bereavement, pain, and woe,
Hallelujah, be it so!   P. M.

69

1 Oh! that on morning's dewy wings
    I from the world might flee away;
And thus escape the bosom-stings
    Fate may inflict some future day.

2 And is it virtue's part to shrink
    From aught that Heaven may ordain?
Shall man, the first and brightest link
    In animated nature's chain,

3 Accept the gifts of grace divine,
    Yet murmur at the mingled ill?
Nor patiently his soul resign
    To God's unalterable will?

4 Mortal! thy impious wish recall,
    Thy spirit arm with fortitude;
Let *guilt alone* thy breast appal,
    Tho' thorns be in thy pathway strewed.

5 Prostrate thyself before the **Lord**,
    Ask not from pain or woe to **fly**;
But that He will that strength accord
    Which triumphs o'er calamity.   P. M.

70

1 Draw nigh, O Lord! unto my soul;
    Compassionate and kind,
Thou only canst the grief control
    Within its depths confined.

2 How long, how deeply I have mourned,
    No human tongue can tell;
For from a heartless world I turned
    To weep but *not rebel*.

3 No! ne'er have I, with lip profane,
    Presumed to ask my God

  Why I the bitter cup should drain,
   Why writhe beneath the rod

4 The hand of Mercy well I knew
  No burthen would impose,
That man's endurance could subdue,
  If faith her aid bestows.

5 Crushed are my hopes, my kindred gone
  Before me to the tomb;
And Thou *alone*, most Holy One,
  Canst dissipate my gloom.

6 The arrow in my bosom lies;
  But stricken hearts have learned,
That oft to " blessings in disguise,"
  Misfortunes have been turned.   P. M.

71

1 I wept when from my eager grasp,
  The hollow toys of fortune fell;
Nor would *that Holy Book* unclasp,
  Where purer, brighter treasures dwell.

2 There came another heavy stroke,—
  Those I loved from earth departed:
Yet were the words religion spoke
  Lost upon the broken-hearted

3 I dared *that* Providence distrust,
  From whom calamities had flowed:
Forgetting, as I bowed to dust,
  Whose hand *past blessings* had bestowed.

4 But suddenly, as from a dream,
  Humbled and self-rebuked I woke:
My spirit then saw Mercy's beam,
  And heard the words that wisdom spoke.

5 How long wilt thou, O child of clay!
   Thy Maker's frown in trials see?
Nor mark His smile in every ray
   That brightens thy prosperity?

6 I wept again; but blest the rod
   Against whose chast'ning I rebelled,
And praised, with equal zeal, my God
   For what He gave and what withheld.

P. M.

72 1 O Thou! in whom the power dwells
   To heal or wound, to save or slay,
Whose hand alone the mandate seals
   That hastens or arrests decay.—
Let me, with pious fortitude,
   Thy dispensations justify,
And in each great vicissitude,
   With perfect faith on Thee rely.

2 Oh ye! who have consigned to dust
   Some darling object of your care,
Fail not in Heaven still to trust,
   Whose Mercy will your loss repair;
Nor let the bitter cup in vain
   Be tendered to your trembling lips:
For God, with beneficial pain,
   Thus of its pride the spirit strips.

3 Mortals presume to call their own
   Blessings vouchsafed by grace divine:
Not as a *gift* but as a *loan*,
   Father! will I consider mine.
And when Thou willest to recall
   All that on earth I love the best,
Before Thy footstool I will fall,
   And bow to Thy supreme behest.

4 The messengers of death surround
   Alike the palace and the cot;
Nor king, nor vassal can be found
   Who shall escape the common lot
Let mighty conquerors declare,
   If they can with disease contend,
Nor in their final struggle share
   The pangs that meaner bosoms rend.

5 Pilgrims! whose aggregate of days,
   With vast eternity compared,
But as a fleeting moment weighs,
   For the last hour be prepared;
Wrestle with sin, watch, worship, praise,
   And glorify the Lord your God,
Who shall to life eternal raise
   The saints that sleep beneath the sod.

                      P. M.

73 1 "Affliction cometh not from dust,
   Nor trouble from the ground;"
But from a Source all-wise and just,
   A God with mercy crowned.

2 The heavy hand from heaven came,
   That on thy heart is pressed;
But, oh? remember 'tis the same
   By which thou oft art blessed.

3 Hast thou, in looking o'er the list
   Of friends and kindred dear,
The names of many loved and missed,
   That were but lately there?

4 O, selfish mourner! weep no more
   For spirits disenthralled,
For those who mortals were before,
   But now are angels called.

5 Wouldst thou, who standest on the brink
   Of the sepulchral sod,
  To suff'ring clay those souls relink
   That have escaped to God?

6 Rather than *lower* these to thee,
   Let faith exalt thy mind,
  In death God's delegate to see,
   Who will the severed bind.

7 All terror from thy thought dismiss:
   For on *His* wings alone
  The righteous leave the grave's abyss,
   To reach their Father's throne.   P. M.

74 1 Healer of the wounded heart!
      Hearer of the mourner's prayer!
     Fortitude to me impart,
      Life's vicissitudes to bear.

2 Let me be possessed alone
   Of the wealth that wisdom yields,
  Such as leads to Heaven's throne,
   Such as virtue's stamp reveals.

3 What is knowledge but the light
   From Omnipotence derived?
  Truth, by whose reflection bright,
   Faith and hope are e'er revived?

4 Grant, O Lord! above all gifts
   Understanding may be mine,
  Such as human nature lifts
   Up to that which is divine.

5 Then what mercy hath decreed
   Will be rightly understood:

That no heart is doomed to bleed
  But for some determined good.   P. M.

75 1 Lord! let Thy countenance now shine
  Upon Thy creature's clouded sense;
That I my spirit may resign
  To all Thou willest to dispense.

2 That, struggling in the depths of woe,
  I may not to despondence yield;
But, while affliction's waters flow,
  Praise my Redeemer, Rock, and Shield.

3 Let sorrow to my stricken heart,
  Through faith, be ever sanctified;
Let grief perform an angel's part,
  And unto Thee the mourner guide.

4 Alas! what fragile props indeed
  Doth human nature rest upon;
Its staff is but a broken reed,
  By death in one brief hour withdrawn.

5 Draw nigh to me, O gracious God!
  No more let my affections cleave
To earth's frail idols, which the sod
  Is ever open to receive.

6 Sire, eternal and supreme!
  To Thee my trembling voice I raise,
Praying Thou wilt with mercy's beam
  Enlighten all my future ways.   P. M.

76 1 Despond not, O my heart!
  But firmly bear thy part
    In life's severe probation;

The path by virtue trod,
Though rugged, leads to God,
　　My Rock and my Salvation.

2　Banish thy secret grief,
Earth's pilgrimage is brief,
　　Its turmoils evanescent:
And when the flesh decays,
God's word the hope conveys,
　　Of happiness incessant.

3　The innocent shrink not
From their appointed lot;
　　But, in the deepest sorrow,
Believe that heaven's light
Follows fate's starless night,
　　To gild the unborn morrow.

4　Lord! though my cares increase,
Oh! grant me inward peace
　　And pious resignation;
Let all I may endure,
Render my spirit pure,
　　And worthy of salvation.　　　　P. M.

77　1　Many are the pains and sorrows
　　Life has yet for me in store;
But from faith my spirit borrows
　　Strength, its trials to endure.
　　Through darkest clouds bright sunbeams break;
Lord! Thou wilt not Thy child forsake!

2　Though falsehood, with envenomed dart,
　　May my innocence assail,

It cannot long affect my heart.
    Shielded by religion's mail,
Nor thence the sweet conviction take,
God ne'er will virtue's cause forsake.

3 Though all I love and cherish sink
    Prematurely in the grave,
In woe I will not cease to think :
    Mercy smiteth but to save.
The dead will in God's kingdom wake ;
The living He will not forsake.

4 Though death in frightful form appear,
    'Gainst my life to lift his scythe,
My mind shall triumph over fear,
    Though the frailer flesh may writhe.
Its perfect trust this cannot shake ;
The faithful God will not forsake.

5 Omnipotent ! *Thou art with me*
    In tears and tribulation ;
Creator ! *I submit to Thee*
    In every dispensation.
My soul Thy essence doth partake ;
This, Father ! Thou wilt not forsake.

P. M.

78

1 When I would smile, remembrance brings
    A thousand sad and bitter things,
Vexations, crosses, wrongs and woes,
That blighted hope and broke repose.
Heavenly Sire ! Holy One !
When shall I say, Thy will be done !

2 I mourned for one who, like a twin,
    Shared every thought that passed within ;

"Oh! would that I might die for thee,"
Was echoed in my agony.
Heavenly Sire! Holy One!
I *should* have said, Thy will be done!

3 Time brought me to the Lord, my Shield,
Whose help my wounds had scarcely healed,
When suff'rings, various and deep,
Destroyed my health and banished sleep;
Heavenly Sire! Holy One!
My words were not, Thy will be done!

4 I saw my kindred's fortunes changed,
The feelings of my friends estranged;
In silence I was doomed to grieve
O'er wants my hand could not relieve.
Heavenly Sire! Holy One!
I said not yet, Thy will be done!

5 How weak in faith must I have been;
How led by sorrow into sin,
In trial ne'er to recognise
The seraph mercy in disguise.
Heavenly Sire! Holy One!
My *heart* now says, Thy will be done!

P. M.

79 1 God of the universe! unfailing friend
Of all who meekly at Thy footstool bend,
In pious gratitude for blessings gained,
Or resignation to the ills ordained,—

2 Oh! grant me firmness in the hour of woe,
To bless the being who has dealt the blow;
And in the furnace, with unceasing prayer,
Avert the evil promptings of despair

3 Hast Thou withdrawn the authors of my
   birth?
  Recalled my dearest kindred from the earth?
  Though nature may her tearful tribute claim,
  Still let the voice of faith exalt Thy name.

4 God of the universe! at Thy command,
  The sun himself and all the starry band
  Shall, like the human frame, at last decay,
  Nor leave, from globes dissolved, one
     ling'ring ray.

5 All, all must perish by progressive blight,
  Or sudden failure of the vital light;
  What unction then shall be to mourners left,
  Of their *material* treasures thus bereft?

6 *Graven on rocks with pen of diamond point*,
  Are words that shall like balm their wounds
     anoint:
  The soul of man o'er ruined worlds shall
     spring,
  And with immortal hosts Thy glories sing.
                                    P. M.

80

1 Frail, feeble, inefficient man!
     In one thing only art thou strong;
  In *will*, to thwart thy Maker's plan,
     In *deed*, to execute the wrong.

2 Unreal glory and false shame,
     By turns thy heart and mind divide;
  The *first* is found in wealth or fame,
     The *last* is only wounded pride.

3 The just who doth the poor redress,
     Below the judge corrupt is placed;

And friends untitled please thee less
　　　　Than strangers that with rank are graced.

4　The majesty of mortal kings,
　　　To thee is ever sanctified;
　　Yet from thy lips arraignment springs
　　　Of God, who doth o'er all preside.

5　O shallow worldling! when they smite,
　　　In silence thou receivest the blow;
　　Yet questionst thy Creator's right
　　　The stroke corrective to bestow.

6　Thou dar'st not in familiar tone
　　　To princes of *this* world appeal;
　　And yet upon the great Unknown
　　　Call lightly in thy woe or weal.

7　The Lord's anointed is not he
　　　Who in a robe of state appears;
　　It is the pious, pure and free,
　　　Whose *spirit* virtue's ermine wears.

8　Frail, feeble, inefficient man!
　　　Oh pray! that thou may'st be ever strong
　　In *will*, to prosecute God's plan,
　　　In *deed*, for e'er to shun the wrong.　P. M.

81

1　My God! my God! to Thee I cling
　　　In sorrow's trying hour;
　　Solace from Thee alone must spring,
　　　Blest and benignant Power!

2　I know there's mercy in the stroke
　　　That bows me to the dust,
　　It frees me from my worldly yoke,
　　　And wakens self-distrust.

3 I feel that faith her tower builds
   On life's most dreary spot;
Her beam the couch of suff'ring gilds,
   And cheers the darkest lot.

4 The wounds that from Thy hand divine,
   In meekness we receive,
The spirit will at last refine,
   And without blemish leave.

5 Boast not, O man! that thou art free
   From salutary pain,
Which well-endured will prove to thee
   A glory and a gain.   P. M.

5. DUTIES TOWARDS OURSELVES.
1. SELF-KNOWLEDGE.

82
1 While man explores, with curious eye,
   The works of nature and of art,
He passeth *real* wisdom by,
   Nor cares to read the human heart.

2 A stranger to himself alone,
   He walketh forth in worldly guise;
Nor wouldst thou in his lofty tone
   The child of frailty recognize.

3 Yet pause, O man! in thy career,
   And search the chambers of thy soul;
For passions dark and deep are there,
   That spurn at reason's weak control

4 A thirst for blood, for gold, for fame,
   Pollutes thee, yet thou know'st it not;
Because it borrows glory's name,
   And sheds false lustre on thy lot.

5 Seek piety—self-knowledge seek,
   Their guidance ask to virtue's road:
On thee will Heaven's light then break,
   And thou wilt know and bless thy God.
                              P. M.

2. SELF-EXAMINATION.

83 1 Descend into thyself, my soul!
   And ask religion's aid
To search thy chambers and control
   The passions there arrayed.

2 E'en from the cradle to the grave,
   God heareth frailty's cry;
Nor can the voice of reason crave
   What Mercy will deny.

3 Oh! ever prone is mortal man
   To self-deceit and sin;
And he who would reform his plan,
   Must turn his eye within.

4 For often vice, with specious art,
   Will virtue's tone affect,
Deceive the sense, deprave the heart,
   And riot there unchecked.

5 Then firmly watch and freely probe
   The slightest moral wound,
And boldly rend deception's robe
   That hides what is unsound.

6 Long hast Thou taught Thy servant, Lord!
   That trust and timely prayer
Will to the spirit strength afford,
   Such discipline to bear.

7 The balm that heals the sinner's hurt
   Springs from a source divine;

O God! regard not my desert,
But let that balm be mine.   P. M.

84

1 Why, O heedless mortal! dost thou fly
So lightly o'er life's rapid stream,
While its shores are briefly passing by,
Like the dim shadows of a dream?
Can thy spirit be a stranger,
To that current's depth and danger?

2 Why, O child of pride! wilt thou not pause,
Earth's tangled pathway to explore?
On to ruin *that* bold pilgrim draws,
Who in his own strength rests secure:
Nor by self-investigation
Arms his senses 'gainst temptation.

3 Daily of myself should I inquire:
Have I fulfilled my being's end?
Is it e'er my heart's supreme desire,
With heaven all its thoughts to blend?
Ah! woe is me! I dare not say
Earth does not lead them far astray.

4 Have I in that first law delighted,
Which doth false gods to man forbid?
Or, while my lip that law recited,
Within my breast some idol hid?
Oh! that I could in truth declare:
One God alone is graven there!

5 Precepts to brotherhood pertaining,
Have I implicitly observed?
Or my poor neighbor's love disdaining,
From God's paternal mandate swerved?
Oh! that I might indeed respond:
I have not broken nature's bond.

6 When felicity was changed to woe,
    Did I still glorify my God?
Or was faith, that man should ne'er forego,
    Relaxed beneath His chast'ning rod?
Alas! my frail and feeble mind
Forgot *past* blessings, and repined.

7 Lord! let this self-examination,
    Answered fore'er in truthful tone,
Lead to the perfect reformation
    Of sin, to which my soul is prone,
And fit it in a future state
With angels to associate.   P. M.

85

1 In glory, Lord! dost Thou appear,
And we the call of angels hear,
The holy praise of Thy great name,
With pious rapture thus proclaim:
              Hallelujah!

2 If in palaces we abide,
Or in rude cottages reside,
Among life's flowers or its weeds,
Still let us strew devotion's seeds.
              Hallelujah!

3 Deep in the heart let virtues dwell,
Like pearls within a mortal shell;
What purer gems for age or youth
Than meekness, innocence, and truth?
              Hallelujah!

4 These weigh not down the spirit's wing
That would to heaven's portal spring;
But speed it in its upward course,
By dint of their own moral force;
              Hallelujah!

5 O Thou! who art the living Fount,
Of mercies man can never count,
From bonds of sin my spirit free,
And let it soar and sing to Thee:
     Hallelujah!

6 No higher privilege I claim
Than to extol Thy blessed name,
And answer, when the angels call,
Holy art Thou, O God of all!
     Hallelujah!
P. M.

2. HUMILITY.

86 1 Hearken not, man! to the voice of self-love;
Adverse to meekness and truth it will prove;
Calling all puny achievements august,
That gild common clay or magnify dust.

2 Wisdom is walking for e'er by thy side,
Checking thy arrogance, chast'ning thy pride,
Bidding thee measure thy fabrics infirm
With works to which time can affix no term.

3 How will thy temples and altars compare
With those that nature delighted to rear?
With the perfect, sublime, and vast designs
Of her forest, ocean, or mountain-shrines?

4 What is thy beauty? the bloom of an hour:
What fame's duration? the life of a flower:
Genius seems ever to sing 'neath a cloud,
Gold cannot brighten *one* thread of the shroud.

5 Self-lauding man! through the firmament's
  bars
  List to the chorus of seraphs and stars:
  Then will thy heart in humility's tone,
  Bow to the world's mighty Master alone.
                                    P. M.

87 1 Out of sorrow's depths I cry
  To my Father, throned on high:
  Mercy's hand, I humbly trust,
  Will remove the mourner's dust,
  While my heart repeats again,
  Bless the Holy One, Amen!

2 Should not I more favor win,
  Than the sons of shame and sin?
  Yet the sweets of life are theirs,
  While my portion is but tears.
  Wherefore have I shouted then,
  Bless the Holy One, Amen?

3 What shall Heaven render *thee*,
  Who thy neighbor's fault canst see,
  Yet art sightless, as the mole,
  To the blots upon thy soul?
  Still unclean, though loud thy strain,
  Bless the Holy One, Amen!

4 He who stands self-justified
  In his spiritual pride,
  Shall no grace from God receive,
  Though he may the world deceive
  By repeating o'er again,
  Bless the Holy One. Amen!   P. M.

GENESIS, CHAP. XI.

88 1 On Shinar's plain see Babel's tower rise:
   Woe shall the builders and their work betide!
For that which seeks to penetrate the skies,
   Shall prove a ruined monument of pride.

2 Here let the bold transgressor read his fate,
   And, trembling, pause amid his plans profane;
Confusion shall upon his deeds await,
   And incomplete his daring schemes remain.

3 Vainly he braves the vengeance of his God:
   For as a moral beacon shall he stand,
While many tongues shall spread his shame abroad,
   His guilt proclaiming through each foreign land.

4 Like lofty towers, haughty hearts shall fall,
   While humble ones to heaven shall aspire,
As they in unity of worship call,
   In death and life, on one Eternal Sire.

P. M.

89 1 My God, my Father, and my Guide!
   On Thee for aid I call;
Oh! save my soul from wordly pride,
   Which causeth man to fall.

2 Power is but a subtle snare,
   Frail spirits to mislead;
Wealth, a treacherous betrayer,
   Fame but a broken reed.

3 Against these lures, Thy servant, Lord!
    For succor hath appealed,
Thou only canst these dangers ward,
    Who art my Strength and Shield.

4 The storm will smite the lofty tree
    That with its rage contends,
But leave the pliant sapling free
    That to its fury bends.

5 So shall the meek, who humbly strive
    Thy wrath to deprecate,
Those blasts of adverse fate survive
    Which shall the proud prostrate.

6 Save Israel from worldly pride,
    All-perfect Source of grace,
And to the gates of heaven guide
    A blind and wandering race!   P. M.

4. CONTENTMENT.

90 1 In the great scales of human life
    God casteth good and ill,
The sweet and bitter, peace and strife,
    By turns the balance fill.

2 Mingled is every mortal draught:
    Yet thus will folly rave:
Wormwood alone have I e'er quaffed,
    My neighbor's cup I crave.

3 His prayer by Providence is heard:
    Doth he the change enjoy?
No! in his heart the gall-drop 's stirred,
    That must all things alloy.

4 His competence enlarged to wealth,
    Brings not expected bliss:
Unsated appetite and health
    Have been exchanged for this.

5 Another of his lot complains,
    Whom all the world thinks blest:
Mere *gold* his lofty soul disdains,
    But sighs for glory's crest.

6 And soon upon his brow august,
    The meed of honor shines;
But ah! his lov'd ones lie in dust,
    For *these* his spirit pines.

7 Take then, O man! the chequered lot,
    To thee by God assigned;
Give thanks for every blessing brought,
    To evil—be resigned.   P. M.

91 1 Oh! whence doth human happiness arise?
Is it dependent upon cloudless skies?
Or on that changeless sunshine of the soul,
That calm content derived from self-control?

2 Light of all seasons, in life's wintry scene,
As in its buoyant spring-time still serene,
Its tempered glory radiates for e'er
From virtue's orbit and religion's sphere.

3 Let us not hope contentment's beam to find
In a restless and ambitious mind;
It rests not on that rainbow of an hour,
The gold and purple robe of worldly pow'r.

4 It gildeth not the godless dome of pride,
Nor in the sordid bosom will abide;

But as the day-star of each mortal shines,
Who in full trust his heart to Heaven
   resigns.

5 O Thou! whose eye all human wants can
   see,
Grant that its influence may govern me;
Let that blest ray of peace my soul illume,
Nor wane till I descend into the tomb.

P. M.

92 1 On dim futurity, with idle aim,
   Man's restless mind is ever prone to gaze,
To know what portion he may chance to
   claim
   Of all the good and ill that fate displays.

2 Impious waste alike of time and thought!
   Insane attempt, that curtain dark to
   rend,
The hand of Providence itself hath wrought,
To veil the evils that o'er life impend.

3 Unwise and rash! foreknowledge, if possest,
   Would aggravate inevitable woe,
Would make the present period unblest,
And crush the nerve that else might
   brave the blow.

4 Thus, too, would promised pleasure lose
   its zest,
   Forestalled by expectation long and keen:
Oh! then let Heaven's wisdom be confest,
That doth from mortal eyes the future
   screen.

5 How grateful is my heart to Thee, O Lord!
  For this concealment of life's chequered
      lines;
  No tongue can utter, and no pen record
    The depth of all Thy merciful designs.
                                                P. M.

PROVERBS, CHAP. XXVII, V. 1.

93 1 Let me for *present* hours borrow
    The garland pleasure wears;
  To God I'll dedicate the *morrow*,
    And mourn for misspent years.

2 Half of thy prayer, to thy own sorrow,
    Is granted, child of mirth!
  The wreath is thine, but e'er the morrow
    'Twill lie with thee in earth

3 The rich man 'neath his purple awning
    Contented sits at eve,
  Nor dreams the sepulchre is yawning,
    His ashes to receive.

4 A widow lifts the voice of mourning,
    For him who yesterday
  Vowed with another sun's returning,
    His pious debts to pay.

5 "The world with graves is perforated,"
    But these beheld them not,
  Their hearts with luxury elated,
    Death's dwelling-place forgot.

6 O Israel! the lesson borrow,
    Nor, for earth's brightest things,
  Defer to an uncertain morrow
    Praise to the King of kings.   P. M.

94 1 Oh! where is he who yesterday
　　Stood erect in manhood's prime?
　Weep! for the shadow of decay
　　Rests upon the child of time;
　Weep for creation's noble chief,
　Whose vital tenure is so brief.

Woe to the man, who in a cloudless morning
　Promise of a golden sunset sees!
Nor heeds experience that whispers warning,
　"Peril lurks in every passing breeze."

2 From the same elements may spring
　　Balm, and bloom, and mortal blight;
　Yet we watch not time's fleet wing,
　　But pursue some vain delight.
　For changing seasons unprepared,
　Though every leaf of life is seared,

O shame! thus to foil our Maker's intent,
　Who moral sagacity gave;
That we might improve to their utmost extent,
　Years that pass between birth and the grave.

3 Waste not the present in regret
　　For omissions of the past;
　Bright blossoms may be gathered yet,
　　Through eternity to last.
　These are virtues—angel flowers,—
　Natives of celestial bowers.

He that to immortality aspires,
　Must his heart to Heaven dedicate,
And all its thoughts, its feelings, and desires,
　By the laws of mercy regulate.　　P. M.

5. FOR THE SICK.

95 1 Hear my voice and grant my pray'r,
    O Thou life-sustaining God!
Heal my flesh, my spirit cheer,
    That I may Thy mercy laud.

2 Trespasses that seemed but light,
    When my health and strength remained,
Now that these have taken flight,
    All the weight of guilt have gained.

3 Oh! that I, in hours past,
    With my soul had oft communed:
Slumb'ring passions thence to cast,
    That awaken but to wound.

4 Lengthen out the little span
    Of Thy worshipper, O Lord!
Nor, till I reform my plan,
    Cleave for e'er the vital cord.

5 As the dial's shadow turned
    At the pray'r of Judah's king,
Let not my appeal be spurned,
    Save me still Thy praise to sing.   P. M.

6. PREPARATION FOR DEATH.

96 1 O thou! possest of health and bloom,
    Think how they once in others glowed;
And yet, how many to the tomb
    Passed, unprepared, to meet their God.

2 Pilgrim! "thy house in order set!"
    Thy soul for sudden change prepare,
Ere thou, to cancel nature's debt,
    Art forced into an unknown sphere.

3 To every fleeting day then link
    Some blest remembrance as it flies,
Some *deed* that on the grave's dark brink
    To soothe thy conscience may arise.

4 Keep mercy ever in thy sight,
    Whether thou judgest friend or foe,
Her mantle, pure as heaven's light,
    Around each erring spirit throw.

5 Let faith triumphant o'er all things.
    Virtue teach and self-denial,
And firmly shall her angel wings,
    Bear thee through life's stormy trial.

6 Mortal! be warned, while yet thy prime
    By dread disease is unassailed;
Oh! trust not to the future time,
    Whose aspect God himself hath veiled.

                              P. M.

6 DUTIES TOWARDS OTHERS.

1. TRUTH.

97 1 Let the standard of truth by Judah be planted,
    Where'er he may chance to abide;
Let praise to the God of his father be chanted,
    Though strangers his worship deride.

2 Oh! fail not to foster each pious emotion
    That reason or faith generates;
But freely and fearlessly breathe your devotion
    To God, who the soul animates.

3 How weak is the sceptre of temporal
    power,
  The spirit of truth to o'erthrow!
Sublimely o'er time doth her majesty tower,
  Eternity's herald below.

4 Her law is a lamp to the feet of each mortal
  That else would in dark places stray;
Its light radiates immortality's portal,
  Nor wanes, though a world may decay.

5 Oh! follow her path, and forsake that of
    error,
  All ye who salvation would seek;
Nor ever, through danger, through shame,
    or through terror,
  Her glorious ordinance break.   P. M.

98

1 Early and late my God I seek,
  Before Him stand and pray;
Yet find all human words too weak
  His wonders to portray.

2 I love to see the morning light
  Break forth to gladden earth,
Like charity, that takes delight
  In cheering humble worth.

3 And when the glorious star of eve
  Ascends the vault on high,
The *first* to reach, the *last* to leave
  Its station in the sky.

4 I think of *Hope*, whose rays serene
  The dawn of life illume,
And still in its decline are seen
  Lingering above the tomb.

5 But brighter, purer, more divine,
　　Is truth than either orb:
　Let this, O God! forever shine,
　　And all my soul absorb.

2. HONESTY.

99 1 Father! will abstinence, or prayer, or song,
　　Open for us celestial portals?
　Or as atonement serve for any wrong
　　Committed 'gainst our fellow-mortals?

2 Oh, no! the key of mercy's golden gates
　　Turns when touched by penitential tears;
　And joy alike the contrite soul awaits,
　　And the meek, that no deep blemish bears.

3 Thou lovest him who faithful, true, and just,
　　Even when by poverty beset,
　Would perish rather than betray his trust,
　　Or the claims of probity forget.

4 The honor Thou as *pure* dost recognise,
　　Builds not on its predecessor's fame;
　Nobility in its *own* spirit lies,
　　Clad in virtue's ermine—a good name.

5 Thy *image* we behold in human love,
　　In human justice trace Thy form divine;
　The soul's high statue, soaring high above
　　All mean artifice and low design.

6 From all that their integrity might blight,
　　God of mercy! Thy weak children shield;
　Most sacred let them hold each other's right,
　　Nor to guileful passions ever yield.

　　　　　　　　　　　　　　P. M.

3. JUSTICE.

DEUTERONOMY, CHAP. I.

100 The prophet to the people said,
    (Whose numbers none might count,)
Full long have ye, O Israel! stayed
    In Horeb's marble mount.

2 Accomplished are your holy wars,
    Ye tread the promised land;
Your multitudes are as the stars:
    God's blessing 's on your band.

3 And may ye, e'en a thousand-fold,
    More numerous become,
On Palestine's conquered mould,
    When ye have fixed your home.

4 But how can I your cumbrance bear,
    Your burthen and your strife?
Wise men among the tribes there are
    To govern ye through life.

5 Let these adjudge the Hebrew's cause,
    The stranger's claim decide,
And in expounding Heaven's laws,
    Heed not the person tried.

6 For in the eye of nature's God,
    Degree no favor finds,
Rank falls 'neath the judicial rod,
    Low as the meanest minds.

7 Of mortal face be not afraid,
    For judgment will descend
From Him who is in truth arrayed,
    The pious poor man's friend.

8 Oh! let the modern Israelite,
　　Taught by the elder time,
　Treasure this golden rule of right,
　　So simple, yet sublime.

9 When ye as arbiters are called
　　Between the small and great,
　Let equity stand unappalled
　　And speak its pure dictate.　　　P. M.

4. RIGHTEOUSNESS.

Psalm XV.

101 Who, God of glory! shall be found
　　Worthy of so high a grace,
　As e'er Thy praises to resound
　　In Thy holy dwelling-place,—
　And with heaven, earth, and sea,
　Join in choral hymns to Thee?

2 He whose soul, all sin abhoring,
　　E'er to virtue's height aspires,
　And 'gainst evil passions warring,
　　Quenches their unholy fires;
　Who 'mid fortune's worst caprice,
　Loses not internal peace.

3 Who shall in the house of prayer,
　　God supreme! Thy praise declare?

　He who with forbearing meekness,
　　Guilt in others palliates,
　Yet in self each lesser weakness
　　Searches out and reprobates.
　He who from reproach or shame
　Guards a fellow-creature's name.

4 Who shall in His holy place
   Praise the Lord of life and grace?

   He whose acts and meditations
      Are alike from falsehood free,
   And of truth, on all occasions,
      Will the fearless champion be.
   Who with life as soon would part,
   As the angel of the heart.

5 Who, O God! is justified
   In Thy temple to abide?

   He who sees in moral duty
      The right tenor of the heart,
   And in holiness a beauty,
      That with time will not depart.
   Virtue thus his soul must raise,
   Who would his Creator praise.   P. M.

5. FORBEARANCE.

102 Of all the virtues that we find
   Promoting bliss among mankind,
   Forbearance, (upon which depends
   The peace of kindred and of friends,)
   Is that which, more than all the rest,
   Conduces to make mortals blest.

   2 Can wit, whose tone is ever high,
      Or beauty that enchants the eye,
      With this domestic grace compare,
      Which doth the robes of meekness wear?
      Whose look serene, and language sweet,
      Rude passion ever can defeat?

   3 Accomplishments, however rare,
      Do not enable us to bear

The wrongs, the trials, and the strife,
To which we are exposed through life;
Or cause us humbly to sustain
Grief, disappointment, want, or pain.

4 No! to this child of faith alone
Are powers of endurance known,—
A sufferance of worldly ill,
A self-denying pious will,
That malice quells, and can assuage
The fiercest mood of frantic rage.

5 Long, long didst *Thou* forbear, O God!
To chasten Israel with Thy rod;
That chosen but rebellious host,
Thy loving kindness never lost.
Be patient still, almighty Sire!
Although their sins provoke Thine ire.

6 Grant me, O ever Just and Wise!
The virtue I most highly prize,
Whose placid temper and soft tone,
I pray henceforth may be my own.
Forbearance grant, in deed and word,
To Thy frail worshiper, O Lord! P. M.

103 Oh! ever adverse to the scheme
  Of Providence divine,
Is proud intolerance, whose beam
  Lights but a single shrine.

2 One creed, one teacher, and one sect,
  Its advocates uphold,
Regardless if a world be wrecked,
  Beyond its narrow fold.

3 It reasons not, but strives to mock
    That charitable zeal,
  That e'en for a dissenting flock,
    Kind sympathy can feel.

4 How patiently hast Thou, O Lord!
    Discordant faiths allowed,
  How equally dispensed reward,
    Or chastisement bestowed:

5 Yet would the bigot sons of pride,
    (Mere bloated worms at best,)
  The movements of man's spirit guide,
    And its free march arrest.

6 Father of mercies! Thou alone
    This blindness canst remove,
  And bring us all before Thy throne,
    In bonds of peace and love. P. M.

104 Why, O man! is not thy soul's desire
      To virtue's excellence confined?
    Why let sinful passions e'er conspire
      To drive her from thy heart and mind!
    So that in earth's most gifted creatures,
    Seldom we mark her modest features.

2 One vain-glorious mortal will pray
    To be with worldly honor crowned;
  And one with the shafts of wit will play,
    Though these the innocent may wound.
  Others there are in the human fold,
  Who ask of Heaven no gift but gold.

3 Shall a righteous neighbor then desert
    The frailest portion of God's flock,

Nor from weak wanderers harm avert,
   Because in evil paths they walk?
Oh! with friendly care and frequent call,
   Watch and warn the erring, lest they fall.

4 Yea, though to the verge of *vice* they stray,
   Your zealous effort ne'er suspend;
Thence, at last they may be led away,
   And made at virtue's shrine to bend.
Pride alone from sinners stands aloof;
Love e'er brings them weeping to her roof.

5 Forbearing Love! patient, gentle, pure,
   On thee the holy task devolves,
Peace to guilty brethren to restore,
   And strengthen penitent resolves;
In each life, however depraved and dark,
Some bright point or moral star to mark.

6 Oh! let man then kindle at that light
   Fire, his base passion to consume;
Then his soul may rise to virtue's height,
   And God's similitude resume.
This blest end forbearance e'er effects,
And human rashness by meek counsel
   checks.   P. M.

GENESIS, CHAP. XLV.

105 What cause hast thou, O Israel, for tears?
The gifts of plenty cheer thy latter years;
And wheresoe'er thine aged feet may rest,
Men shall rise to honor and call thee blest.

2 Ah, woe is me! the patriarch repeats,
   Since he no more his darling Joseph
      greets.

In sorrow to the grave must I go down,
Nor peace, nor happiness my gray hairs
  crown.

3 And where was he, lamented thus as lost?
From pit and prison up to honor's post;
Heaven progressively the wand'rer led,
To bless the hands that would his blood
  have shed.

4 His dreams of stars and sheaves are
    realized;
Awhile his deep emotions are disguised,
When at his foot-stool all his brethren fall,
And upon Egypt's lord for succor call.

5 I am that man, that brother whom ye sold!
Say, does my father live? Would I might
    fold
Within my arms that parent well-beloved,
Whose partial tenderness your envy
    moved!

6 Yet, fear ye not! regret alone I feel,
Ye against nature should your bosom steel;
The hand of Mercy we may here detect,
From evil cause producing good effect.

7 O ye! who with vindictive anger burn,
Forbearance now from this example learn;
Forgive your foes, and in the part delight,
Their injuries with kindness to requite.
                                    P. M.

6. BROTHERLY LOVE.

106 How beautiful it is to see,
Brethren unite harmoniously!

Of kindred sympathies possest,
By the same joys and woes imprest.

2 But ah! how very slight a cause,
Will counteract kind nature's laws,
And to that dread estrangement lead,
Against which God and angels plead!

3 An unkind word, pronounced in haste,
Hath years of tenderness effaced,
Checked confidence, whose genial flow
Is sweeter than aught else below.

4 In jealousy a poison lurks,
That oft affection's ruin works;
This first implants suspicion's seeds,
And to fraternal contest leads.

5 Ye brothers, who would cherish strife,
Oh, think of those who gave you life!
By whom ye were together blest,
Watched, prayed for, counseled and
    carest;

6 What deep reproach to these it bears,
What grief entails on their gray hairs,
When discord on their household band,
Hath laid a cold and with'ring hand!

7 Lord of the universe! we pray,
Thou wilt this evil put away,
And grant that Israel may be found,
In faith by concord ever crowned.   P. M.

107 "Let there be love!" it is the light
That makes the sphere of heaven bright.
First, from creative Mercy's thought,
By the rejoicing angels caught.

2 "Let there be love!" it is the beam
   That earth from darkness shall redeem,
   And in its mighty heart mature
   The only bud that shall endure.

3 "Let there be love!" its vital ray,
   Alone exempt from brief decay,
   Shall in the human soul entomb
   The germ of its immortal bloom.

4 "Let there be love!" its gentle tone
   Is music heard from Mercy's throne,
   Echoed by charity below
   To hush the cry of guilt or woe.

5 "Let there be love!" blest is the creed
   That doth to this pure issue lead,
   And thus promotes the hallowed plan
   Of brotherhood 'twixt man and man.

6 "Let there be love!" earth, air, and sea,
   Obedience yield to this decree;
   Woe then to reason froward child!
   Whose spirit is by *hate* defiled.

7 O God! let universal love,
   Unholy strife from earth remove,
   And link, in one harmonious whole,
   All human kind from pole to pole.   P. M.

108 Truly and tenderly should I
    As myself my neighbor love,
His weal promote, his wants supply,
    And with him in concord move.
Thus by God's benign command,
Clasping close the social band.

2 For this did Providence decree,
   From the cradle to the tomb,
None from sorrow should be free,
   But partake one common doom;
That the tried and suffering heart
Might kind sympathy impart.

3 The poor, the rich, the meek, the proud,
   Side by side our Father placed,
Each with reason's power endowed,
   Each with His own image graced.
Who shall then with selfish aim,
Mock at man's fraternal claim?

4 Will destiny, that through the globe
   Flings for e'er its iron barb,
More venerate the monarch's robe
   Than the beggar's tattered garb?
With hand impartial, it will strike
Pride and poverty alike!

5 Oh! wherefore then as strangers treat
   Pilgrims seeking the *one* road,
That leads them to the mercy-seat
   Of a universal God?
Who alone beyond life's goal,
Shall distinguish soul from soul.

6 Men, who live on earth as brothers,
   There shall find a Father's love;
And the tears *here* wept for others,
   There shall pearls of ransom prove,
Mortal frailties to redeem
From the wrath of the Supreme.   P. M.

7. FILIAL LOVE.
Exodus, chap. xx., v. 13.

109
When I remember, O my God!
  The bounties from my birth received,
Knowledge that from my *parents* flowed,
  Of all Thy mercies had achieved:

2 Those guardians, how shall I requite,
    Who cherished me thro' childhood's
        stage?
  Unless I in Thy law delight,
    And shield and honor them in age;

3 Soften with unremitting care,
    Frailties they may through life betray,
  With love and reverential fear,
    Their least command or wish obey.

4 Ye outcasts from the social pale!
    Apostates from the filial creed!
  Let Sinai's warning voice prevail,
    When nature fails her cause to plead.

5 Bless ye the authors of your birth,
    Next to your heavenly Father's praise,
  The highest duty upon earth,
    That faith enjoins or man obeys. P. M.

110
Intensely radiant was thy peak,
  Majestic Horeb! on the day
That moral light was seen to break
  On Israel's benighted way.
    Hallowed sod!
    Where a *God*
Through His delegate conveyed
Laws in mercy's spirit made.

2 List, O ye children of the earth!
    List to the mandate of the Lord!
Honor the sources of your birth,
    And with your love their care reward.
        These defend
      To life's end,
Nor your filial task relax
Till the grave its prey exacts.

3 Let grateful memory look back
    To infancy's dependent hours,
Who drew you through its thorny track,
    And taught you where to find its
        Parent hearts   [flowers?
      By soft arts,
Safe your steps through peril led,
And life's roses 'neath them spread.

4 Nature's voice, to you appealing,
    Claims return for past protection,
Guarding, both by faith and feeling,
    This her holiest affection.
        Ne'er forget
        Her just debt;
But, while with existence blest,
Fond devotion manifest.

5 O Lord! Thy choicest blessing yield
    To our loved parents while they live;
And when in death their eyes are sealed,
    Their souls receive, their sins forgive.
      From the grave,
      Father! save
Those who trained us, from early youth,
To know and love the laws of truth.

                                    P. M.

8. MATRIMONIAL LOVE.

111
Blest is the bond of wedded love,
   When they who at its altar bow,
Remember that the God above
   Is witness to their holy vow,—

2 When they sweet counsel interchange,
   And as each season onward rolls,
Prove that no chance can e'er estrange
   The feeling that unites their souls.

3 To woman, in the stormy hour,
   Doth not her stronger partner turn?
And from her spirit gather power,
   Peril and pain alike to spurn?

4 And she, the gentle, tender one,
   Whose atmosphere is purity,—
Doth she not in *his* love alone
   Confide for her security?

5 That noble trust, O man! fulfill,
   Which before Heaven hath been sworn;
Cherish thy wife through good and ill,
   Her virtues love, her frailties mourn.

6 Blest are the vows of wedded life,
   When they from righteous lips proceed,
When free from wrath, perverseness, strife,
   Time hallows that which God decreed.
                    P. M.

9. CHARITY.

112
O thou, whose shrine the sweetest incense
   bears
Which human gratitude for God prepares,

Exalted charity! in whom we trace
Mercy's twin-attribute and sister grace,
Thy name we glorify, thy praise prolong,
Whose power changeth mourning into song.

2 'Tis thine, benevolence! with soft control,
To draw the arrow from the stricken soul,
To fly unbidden to thy brother's aid,
And balm the wound by cruel fortune made,
O'er widowed worth thy shelt'ring wings to spread,
And cheer the drooping children of the dead.

3 Oft by the cypress of the parent's tomb
The orphan's bud of hope is seen to bloom;
Thy smile the beam, thy tear the gentle dew,
That brighter make the infant-blossom's hue.
Oh! not less kind shall mercy prove above
To those who follow *here* her law of love.

P. M.

Prov., chap. xiv., 11.

113 I saw a palace proud and high,
A work that vanity had planned,
Its towers pointed to the sky,
Not so its master's heart or hand.

2 There stood an humble mansion near,
And wisdom was its architect,

Pillars of holiness were there,
  While charity its portals decked.

3 And worldly men, as these they past,
  Would linger long before the first,
 But **looked** with scorn upon the **last**,
  As though it were a thing accursed.

4 Behold! a bolt from heaven falls
  And blasts the rich man's residence;
 While from its neighbor's lowly walls
  Rise songs of praise to Providence.

5 That house is built on **barren sand**
  In which faith's treasures are **not stored**;
 Nor **long** shall any fabric stand
  Whose founder feareth not the Lord.

P. M.

JOB, CHAP. XXIX.

114 Return, **O Lord!** and let me be
  As I have been in seasons past,
 When, graciously preserved by Thee,
  No shadow on my soul was cast.

2 When firm and fearless in my youth,
  Through darkness oft I walked abroad,
 Wanting no star but perfect truth,
  No sun to light me, but my God,

3 Where are the troops of flatterers **now**,
  Who once my tabernacle sought?
 No word of comfort they bestow
  Upon a heart with anguish fraught.

4 The poor in me a father hailed,
  And freely of my stores partook;
 But since my earthly treasures failed,
  E'en *these* my presence cannot brook.

5 Proud men and princes held their peace,
   When I for justice raised my voice,
And caused the orphan's tear to cease,
   The widow's spirit to rejoice.

6 Yea, righteousness hath been my robe,
   And equity my diadem;
Yet, scorners seek my wounds to probe,
   And my integrity condemn.

7 Oh! blest be he who, when bereaved
   Of worldly substance, children, friends,
Finds balm in former good achieved,
   And with his prayer no murmur blends.

                              P. M.

115 Bounteous Father! by what course
   May we hope Thy grace to gain?
Oh! must we not, in active force,
   All Thy laws of love maintain?

2 Linked alike in mind and heart,
   Should not all Thy creatures live?
Bidding revenge and hate depart,
   And delighting to forgive?

3 Ne'er, O man! this charge forego;
   But with unaffected zeal,
E'en an erring brother's woe,
   Strive with gentle hand to heal.

4 Doth he wear the prisoner's bond?
   Seek him in his dark abode,
Show what beams from spheres beyond,
   Light the weeping pilgrim's road.

5 Art thou with ease and comfort blest,
   While he languishes in need?

Cast in the field of barrenness,
   Part of fortune's golden seed.

6 Welcome poor earth-mates to thy roof,
   Share with **these** thy **daily bread**;
Our Father never stands aloof
   While His children thus are fed.

7 When thy hearth-stone brightly gloweth,
   There to love an altar rear,
That which Providence bestoweth,
   For its sacrifice prepare.

8 Wouldst thou please thy heavenly Sire?
   Let thy *mite* precede thy *meal;*
Grace like *this* ascendeth higher
   Than the lips' prescribed appeal.

9 Be to the lame a strong support,
   For the blind thine eyes exert:
And the angels then shall make report
   Of thy glorious desert.

10 Faith ever in its sacred scope
    Sweet charity embraces,
And on it man's eternal hope
    By God's commandment bases.   P. M.

Psalm XLI.

116 Oh! blest be he who ne'er forgets the poor,
But with the needy freely shares his store;
Upon the bed of languishing and pain,
He shall not call upon the Lord in vain;
For him, who doth a *brother's* anguish feel,
A *Father's* hand shall strengthen then, and
   heal.

2 That man's name on earth shall never
    perish,
Who doth the widow cheer, the orphan
    cherish,
Who with integrity has treasures earned,
That to the use of charity are turned:
Time shall repeat his deeds through future
    years,
And angels sing them in celestial spheres.

3 But, oh! let none of those who practice
    fraud,
Believe they can propitiate their God,
By placing in the beggar's outstretched
    hand,
Gold gathered up by breach of his command.
E'en mercy will refuse *his* gift to bless,
Who 'gainst the laws of justice doth trans-
    gress.

4 Let all who would their Maker's love
    requite,
Beneficence with probity unite.
He who created pure the human heart,
Meant not that these should ever dwell
    apart;
His bounty Providence will ne'er approve,
Who dares his neighbor's landmark to
    remove.   P. M.

117 Stretched languidly upon his couch,
    The child of pomp seeks rest,
While those who round his chamber crouch,
    Believe him truly blest.

2 From these the curtained sluggard hid,
    Seems wrapped in mimic death,
 They cannot see his unclosed lid,
    Nor mark his panting breath.

3 Of precious balsams sleep alone
    Baffles his costly bribe;
 Balm to the temperate e'er known,
    And to the toiling tribe.

4 And cannot affluence indeed
    This priceless gift possess?
 Yes! of the orphan's tear take heed,
    The widow's wrong redress.

5 Call famished brethren to thy board,
    And in their blessings taste
 A luxury wealth ne'er procured
    In all its boundless waste.

6 The work of charity begin
    That selfish ease foregoes;
 The poor man's prayer for thee shall win
    Serene and sweet repose.

7 Body and soul beneath thy sway
    Shall healthful vigor gain,
 And slumber, chased by sloth away,
    Come to thy couch again.   P. M.

118 Pray in the night! when silence and the stars
    Alone bear witness to thy holy zeal;
 And when the morn removes light's golden bars,
    Praise Nature's God who heareth man's appeal.

2 For praise, like manna, ever is most sweet,
   Ere yet the spirit, like the noontide sun,
Wax in its worldly course to that fierce heat
   By which corruption's fatal work is done,

3 And if the measure of thy blessing prove
   More ample than thy neighbor's lot contains,
Forget not Heaven's ordinance of love,
   But yield to him a portion of thy gains.

4 So shall the sons of Israel regain
   The love of God long forfeited by guile;
Like a relenting father will He deign
   Once more on contrite worshipers to smile.   P. M.

Prov. XIII., v. 7.

119 How oft has man, with "heart of stone,"
   The gifts of Providence received,
Nor felt they were but Mercy's loan,
   That good through him might be achieved.

2 Wrapt in himself he will not see
   That, as the Lord's appointed steward,
He must dispense, with spirit free,
   Treasures ne'er meant to be immured.

3 Whence does all mortal strength proceed,
   If not from wealth? the boaster cries;
No privilege can nature need,
   Or thought suggest, that gold denies.

4 Oh! false and fatal estimate
   Of specious, unsubstantial dross

Which cannot ward *one* stroke of faith,
    Or lighter make affection's loss.

5 Its glitter mocks the coffin-plate
    Where life's epitome is traced;
Can it redeem *one* evil trait
    By which the soul has been debased?

6 Impassive lies the frozen heart,
    Till care or woe its current thaws;
Nor till its brighter hopes depart,
    Will bow to love's benignant laws.

7 Children of opulence! reflect,
    That ye from God *your pensions* gained,
And, as His almoners elect,
    Share with the poor the gifts obtained.

                            P. M.

V. MISCELLANEOUS HYMNS.

1. FAITH, HOPE, AND LOVE.

120 Who is that angel of the universe,
    That *first* and purest spiritual grace,
Through whom alone man may with God
        converse,
    And with a tear his trespasses efface?
That gentle spirit who, when stricken saith,
God's holy will be done? 'Tis faith, meek
    faith!

2 Who is that *second* messenger divine,
    That 'mid life's stormy elements suspendeth

A bow, a promise—an eternal sign,
　That Heaven's mercy e'er its wrath
　　transcendeth?
Not long can sorrow its deep fountains ope
Before *that* seraph. It is hope, sweet hope!

3 Lo! a *third* angel to the earth repairs,
　Kindred to both of these celestial powers;
Religion's self its oracle declares,
　And finds its essence in all mortal
　　flowers.
The mourner's heart to rapture it can
　　move,—
Its voice is melody. Its name is love!

4 Welcome, ye angels of the universe!
　Welcome, faith, hope, and love, to Israel's
　　tents!
Ye who the shadows of the soul disperse,
　And peace and gladness to the world
　　dispense.
With song we praise each spiritual grace
That links immortals to the human race.
　　　　　　　　　　　　P. M.

2. PRAYER.

121 Pray when the morn unveileth
　Her glories to thine eyes;
Pray when the sun-light faileth,
　And stars usurp the skies,
Far from my bosom flinging
　Each worldly thought impure,
The praise of God be singing,
　Mortal! for evermore.

2 Pray for the friend whose kindness
   Ne'er failed in word or deed;
Pray for the foe whose blindness
   Hath caused thy heart to bleed.
A blessing for thy neighbor
   Ask thou of God above;
And on thy hallowed labor
   Shall fall His smile of love.

3 Beside the **stranger's altar**,
   Or at thy proper **shrine**,
Let not thy accents falter
   In utt'ring truths divine.
But e'en when life is waning,
   Thy faith with zeal declare—
One God alone is reigning
   Whose worship none may share

P. M.

122 When night from nature's kingdom flies,
Let prayer and light together rise;
For prayer shall, like the **morning beam**,
From darkness e'en thy soul redeem.

2 **No** *worldly service* should precede
   The praise of *Him* whose will decreed
That sleep should like the dew descend,
   And freshness **to** life's flower lend.

3 Present thy spirit before God,
   Unsullied by the mortal load
Of follies, passions, crimes, and cares,
Earth for her weary sons prepares.

4 Thy heart before *His* eye unmask,
  And crave a blessing on thy task,
  Strongly shalt thou be fortified
  To wrestle then with scorn and pride.

5 Then, when the sleep of death is near,
  And thou hast said thy farewell prayer,
  In *prospect*, pilgrim, shalt thou see
  The sunrise of eternity.   P. M.

123 Though faith's discordant worshipers may rear
  A thousand shrines, and cherish creeds diverse,
  Yet harmonize they in regarding prayer
  As virtue's guardian and religion's nurse.

2 Prayer is the only universal tongue
  Familiar both to the refined and rude;
  Incense on household altars daily flung
  From the o'erflowing urn of gratitude.

3 Prayer is the valve made for the heart's relief
  From all that pride hath in its depths concealed;
  'Tis the securest vent for smothered grief
  For hopes long damped and sorrows never healed.

4 Prayer is of Heaven's bond the holy seal,
  That man with God may hold high intercourse,
  Who hears and answers ev'ry pure appeal,
  Whether of righteousness or true remorse.

5 Sweet is the voice of childhood when it
    pleads
  For earthly parents to its Sire above,
When with unsullied lips it intercedes
  To win for them His blessing, grace,
    and love.

6 And oh! how solemn are the prayers of age,
    When all the vanities of earth are fled;
  How tremblingly it turns the holy page,
    And prays to God who raiseth up the
      dead.

7 First balm of youth, last unction of the old,
    Thy efficacy mortals shall attest,
  Till life's last breath in prayer becometh
    cold,
  And the long burthened spirit sinks to
    rest.   P. M.

124 In perilous probation here
      Were ye, O mortals! sent
    For future being to prepare
      Of infinite extent.

2 The soul against the flesh contends
    For its immortal right;
  Victorious, when faith descends
    To aid its upward flight.

3 But, if temptation's voice ye hear,
    Persuasive, strong and sweet,
  And strive not then by fervent prayer
    Her power to defeat.

4 Then will the earth-bound spirit fall,
    Degraded and supine,
And at the carnal tempter's call
    Its heritage resign.

5 Likeness to God man's features boast,
    Reflected in the *soul;*
But this similitude is lost
    'Neath sensual control.

6 Back to heaven whence it came,
    Let it return again,
Unsullied by the brand of shame,
    Or sin's deep-seated stain.   P. M.

3. DIVINE WORSHIP.

125 Oh, worship God! approach His shrine,
    All ye children of the dust;
Exalt that Providence divine
    In whose guardianship ye trust.
Are ye the affluent? Alas!
    Wealth preserves ye not from woe;
Care e'en through palace gates will pass,
    Bribes suspend not death's strong blow.

2 Oh, worship God! His temple seek,
    Helpless offspring of despair!
Advance, ye languishing and weak!
    To the nursery of prayer.
Has fortune crushed beneath her wheel,
    Those she once with riches crowned?
Has friendship, that her wounds should heal,
    Left your bleeding hearts unbound?

3 Oh, worship God! His name extol,
    Who man's lot hath equalized,
Causing proud opulence to fall,
    Raising needy worth despised.
Forget not then, ye righteous poor,
    Though ye taste not of the sweets
With which your brother's cup runs o'er,
    Justice still each portion metes.

4 Worship the Lord, ye widowed hearts!
    Whose promise faith hath spoken,
Who balm to the bereaved imparts,
    And soothes the spirit broken.
Ye fatherless! your grief assuage,
    And to God address your prayers;
The shield of youth, the staff of age,
    Gently dries the orphan's tears.

5 Worship your Maker, sons of earth!
    In plenty or privation;
Though high or humble be your birth,
    Lofty or low your station.
In kindness oft life's bitter draught
    To human lips is tendered;
Let homage, e'en while it is quaffed,
    To God be meekly rendered.   P. M.

126 Lift, lift the voice of praise on high,
The Lord of life to glorify!
Thy spirit bow in humble prayer,
Remember, mortal, God is here.

2 Within the sanctuary's walls,
    To dust all proud pretension falls;

    The curtain of the soul is drawn,
    And worldly vanities are gone.

3 Art thou in power's highest place?
   Oh! turn towards the throne of Grace;
   How will thy fancied grandeur fleet
   Before thy Maker's mercy-seat.

4 Dost thou of temp'ral treasures boast?
   Faith slumbers not upon her post,
   But asks thee, with impressive tone,
   How thou repayest Heaven's loan.

5 If want, by thee unaided, weeps,
   Nor gleanings from thy harvest reaps,
   Then art thou poor, with all thy gold,
   For virtue casts thee from her fold.

6 Oh! may our thoughts, eternal God!
   Be suitable to Thy abode;
   These disengage from sordid schemes,
   And wean from all ambition's dreams.

7 Let holiness alone pervade
   The soul by Thee immortal made;
   And grant that, till its final flight,
   Thy praise may prove its chief delight.
                                P. M.

127 Here, at this temple's holy shrine,
      Let Israel join in sacred prayer,
   And every thought to Him resign
      Who sheds on us His tender care:
   Then hearts sincere in grateful praise
   Shall sanctify the hymns we raise.

2 Oh! let not pride nor envy dwell
   Where righteousness alone should reign,
That sweet religion's holy spell
   May lead us back to grace again;
And all be most supremely blest
Who bow before His high behest.

3 Pure is the soul which God hath made,
   Let sin's deep stain defile it not,
That, when our mortal debt is paid,
   And earthly cares in death forgot,
To realms of endless bliss it flies,
Eternal rest beyond the skies.　　C. M. C.

4. DEVOTION.

128 Refuge I seek at the shrine of devotion,
   When life's evil destinies compass me round,
There can my heart ever calm its commotion,
   By prayers poured forth from its innermost ground.

2 Those who in smiles and in sunshine are basking,
   Listen but coldly to sorrow's rehearsal;
Witness *Thou only* my spirit's unmasking,
   Father of mercy and Friend universal.

3 Thou, by whose hand every wound is anointed,
   Wilt (as thy servant each weakness confesses)
Give to the heart, of its hope disappointed,
   Counsel that chastens not less than it blesses.

4 Grant me, great Fountain of faith and of
    feeling!
  Patient endurance and meek self-denial,
  Give to the soul at Thy altar appealing,
    Courage in peril and firmness in trial.

P. M.

129 Begin the holy hymn of praise,
    And let the choral band
  Repeat, as they their voices raise:
    Know before whom ye stand!

2 All ye in convocation brought
    By God's divine command,
  Remember what His hand hath wrought:
    Know before whom ye stand!

3 'Tis He whose ark the deluge braved,
    Whose rainbow heaven spanned,
  Whose outstretched arm the righteous
    saved:
  Know before whom ye stand!

4 The self-revealed, the great *I AM*,
    Who lead from Egypt's land
  The heirs of faithful Abraham:
    Know before whom ye stand!

5 Who sent to Bethel (house of God)
    A glorious angel band
  To bless the dreamer on the sod:
    Know before whom ye stand!

6 Though now the glory may be lost,
    That God for Judah planned,

Forsake not faith's exalted post:
　　Know before whom ye stand!

7　Oh! let devotion, pure and strong,
　　　Your grateful hearts expand,
　　Repeating still in sacred song:
　　　Know before whom ye stand!　　　P. M.

5　PRAISE AND THANKSGIVING.

Psalm CL.

130　Praise ye the Lord! for it is good
　　　His mighty acts to magnify,
　　And make those mercies understood,
　　　His hand delights to multiply.
　　　　Praise ye the Lord!

2　Break forth, O Israel! into song,
　　　Let hymns ascend to heaven's vault;
　　No sweeter task hath mortal tongue,
　　　Than its Creator to exalt.
　　　　Praise ye the Lord!

3　The firmament's bright starry wall
　　　Shall tremblingly vibrate the sound,
　　When with a trumpet ye extol
　　　A God who doth in grace abound.
　　　　Praise ye the Lord!

4　Smite ye the harp, the timbrel roll,
　　　And let the organ swell sublime
　　In praise of Him who formed the soul
　　　For bliss beyond the bounds of time.
　　　　Praise ye the Lord!

5 O holy, holy, holy King!
    Prostrate we bow before Thy throne,
And of salvation's power sing,
    Possessed by *Thee*, and *Thee alone*.
  Praise ye the Lord!

6 Let hallelujah loudly rise!
    Let hallelujah softly fall!
Until on angel lips it dies,
    As they unto each other call,
  Praise ye the Lord!   P. M.

131 Let the Lord be ever praised,
    Ever loved and glorified;
Though His mighty hand be raised,
    Sons of earth to bless or chide.

2 Wisdom, justice, truth, and grace,
    Are His attributes sublime;
These are seen throughout all space,
    These are felt throughout all time.

3 Contemplate, O mortal man!
    Heaven and its starry host,
Worlds of light, whose perfect plan
    Leaves the soul in wonder lost.

4 Turn and view the elements,
    In their calmness or their strife,
Ocean, that appals the sense,
    Air, that ministers to life.

5 Earth, that, while thou livest, yields
    All her fruitful breast contains,
When thou diest, kindly shields
    All of thee that then remains.

6 Last, the restless flame behold,
    As it towers to the clouds,
Bursting through its smoky fold,
    Like thy spirit from its shrouds.

7 Seest thou not in all of these
    Emanations, pure and bright,
From that Power whose decrees
    Can alone bring bloom or blight?

8 Seek not then, whate'er thy state,
    Whether lofty or obscure,
Mysteries to penetrate,
    But be silent and adore.

                                    P. M.

132 O uncreated Holy One!
Lowly we bow before Thy throne,
Seeking salvation from above,
We praise Thy name with songs of love.
    Hallelujah! hallelujah! Amen!

2 Forgive us, Father! hear our cry,
Oh! let us not in darkness die;
Remove from us our moral night,
And bless us with a ray of light.
    Hallelujah! hallelujah! Amen!

3 O King of kings! O Fount of life!
Turn us from all that leads to strife;
Beneath the shadow of Thy wing,
Let us our hymns in glory sing.
    Hallelujah! hallelujah! Amen!

                                    C. D. L. H.

133 Eternal, almighty, invisible God!
We gratefully enter Thy sacred abode,
With rev'rence and love to exalt Thy great
   name,
And loudly thy manifold mercies proclaim.

2 As kindred surrounding a family shrine,
We here stand assembled for worship
   divine;
Thy presence, O Lord! let us all realize,
While songs to Thy throne shall in har-
   mony rise.

3 Though angels their voices with mortals
   unite,
And sing of Thy glory from morning to
   night;
All praises must short of Thy excellence
   fall,
Creator, Protector, and Father of all!

4 Oh! still be the Shepherd of Israel's flock,
Progressive in faith let us steadily walk,
Made pure by Thy law, to whose promise
   and threat
The seals, both of justice and mercy were
   set.

5 Blest witnesses shall we continue to be,
That we have no god nor redeemer but
   Thee,
Thy truth and Thy unity zealous to urge,
In life or when brought to eternity's verge.

                                   P. M.

134 We bless Thee, O Lord! as the bountiful Source
Of gifts which the seasons renew in their course;
For the showers of *Spring*, whose verdure and bloom
Are redeemed by Thy hand from a wintry tomb.

2 In *Summer departed*, the Lord, our Shield,
To man all the glory of nature revealed,
The light of whose spirit past over the earth,
Undimmed by the shadows of sickness or dearth.

3 Thy mercy, O God! let the living extol,
When the leaves of the *Autumn* around them fall,
Who still with the fruits of abundance are crowned,
While death for his sickle no harvest hath found.

4 Thou wilt not forsake in the *Winter* of age,
The righteous who praised Thee in life's early stage.
The sacrifice, then, of thanksgiving ne'er cease,
All ye who are blessed with health, freedom, and peace.

5 A few may yet weep in the fullness of love,
For those whom Thy wisdom thought fit to remove;

Grieve not when a child in its purity dies,
From dust as a cherub it soon shall arise.

6 Nor long mourn for those who, maturer in
   years,
Before us have passed from the valley of
   tears;
Though dead to this world, in a brighter
   abode
They dwell with their Father, their Friend,
   and their God.   P. M.

135 Extol the King who, throned above,
And crowned with righteousness and love,
Hath reigned from the eternal past,
And shall be Sovereign to the last.

2 His praise the morning sun began,
Ere he the course of nature ran,
When conscious of a glow divine,
In majesty he rose to shine.

3 His praise the stars of evening sung,
When they into their orbits sprung,
And filled the firmament of night,
With glory from a greater light

4 And earth to its remotest bound,
Still circulates the joyous sound,
Rock, wave, and wind, and tree, and flow'r,
Confess an omnipresent Pow'r.

5 Art thou alone, O mortal man!
A silent witness of that plan,
By wisdom and by mercy wrought,
That faith might to thy soul be taught?

6 Arise! and with thy heart and voice,
In presence of thy God rejoice!
For thought and speech to thee belong,
For meditative praise and song.
P. M.

136 All living souls shall bless Thy name,
   O just and gracious God!
All flesh Thy providence proclaim,
   Thy holy works applaud.

2 From age to age will we relate
   The wonders Thou hast wrought,
Delighting to expatiate
   On all which Thou hast taught.

3 Young men and maidens lift the voice,
   Thy wisdom to extol;
And children in Thy praise rejoice,
   Father and Friend of all!

4 But though our hands should be outspread,
   As are the eagle's wings,
To thank Thee for the daily bread,
   That from Thy bounty springs;

5 Though song, like sounding billows, too,
   Should from our lips proceed;
How large a debt would yet be due
   To Thee, from Jacob's seed!

6 Thrice holy, Lord of hosts! art Thou,
   Ineffable and pure!
Before Thy Majesty we bow,
   Great King, whom we adore.
P. M.

137
Above all honor and all praise,
  Art Thou exalted, Lord!
Yet would our lips in holy lays,
  Glory to Thee accord.

2 Thy truth transcendeth human thought,
    Thy love no limit knows;
  And every precept Thou hast taught,
    With mercy's spirit glows.

3 Time hath for Thee no present hour,
    No past or future day;
  Eternity attests Thy pow'r,
    And mocks his measured sway.

4 Though brief our mortal period,
    Let us that knowledge gain,
  Which brings us near to Thee, O God!
    And bursts our worldly chain.

5 Oh! let it be our chief delight,
    From carnal links to free
  The soul, whose essence, pure and bright,
    Claims kindred, Lord! with Thee.
P. M.

138
Glory and praise to the bountiful Sire,
Whose hand gave to man all his heart
    could desire,
  Placed organs of speech in the temple of
      thought,
  And the music of prayer from the soul
      thus brought.

2 O beautiful harmony! spirit and voice

In the praise of their maker together
  rejoice,
His name magnify and His attributes laud,
Past, present, and future—the One, only
  God!

3 Sing, Israel! sing of that Power Supreme.
  Whose wisdom reflecting its own chastened
    beam,
  On the image of clay upon which it had
    breathed,
  To mortals the blessing of reason
    bequeathed.

4 O ineffable gift! unparalleled grace!
  Let it ring through all time, resound
    through all space,
  That star of the mind virtue's course
    indicates,
  And truth's holy light in its orb
    concentrates.

5 And though no conception or language of
    ours,
  E'en faintly may shadow God's presence or
    powers;
  Let us never forego the music of prayer,
  Nor anthems of praise that His mercies
    declare. P. M.

139 House of Judah, bless the Lord!
  Let His praise be your delight;
On your hearts His law record,
  Walk ye in its perfect light.

2 Let the poor an altar rear,
    Though with roughest stones they build;
  If the worship be sincere,
    Faith's high purpose is fulfilled.

3 Round that unpretending shrine,
    Angel visitants shall stand;
  'Tis a bethel as divine,
    As the Luz of holy land.

4 By the rich, who oft to pride
    Cedar palaces erect,
  Temples should be multiplied
    Like the fane that Zion decked.

5 Yet, if sacrifice in these
    Rise not up from righteous folds,
  It will fail that God to please
    Who but asks *unblemished souls*.

6 Bless the Lord, ye rich and poor!
    E'en as brothers, bless One Sire;
  Love fraternal, meek and pure,
    Feeds devotion's altar-fire.   P. M.

140 If mortal vision may not meet
    The sun's meridian rays;
  But would beneath some cloud retreat,
    To shun its noontide blaze:

2 Oh! how shall man then elevate
    The soul's eternal eye
  To God, the awful aggregate
    Of suns that never die?

3 In whom the lights of truth and grace,
    Of wisdom, justice, love,
In one stupendous mind embrace,
    And in one glory move?

4 As angels cover with their wings,
    Their dazzled orbs on high,
Friendly to faith, kind nature flings
    'Twixt God and man the sky.

5 Softly the veil thus interposed,
    Relieves the spirit's gaze,
And lips that e'er in fear had closed,
    Now ope, the Lord to praise.

6 Reflective of Almighty beams,
    The soul intensely burns,
And ever most immortal seems,
    When heavenward it turns.   P. M.

141 Princes of earth! bend lowly down
    Before the Lord of hosts,
Who sees in holiness a crown,
    More bright than monarch boasts.

2 And ye, who o'er the free preside
    With delegated sway,
Ask counsel of that gracious Guide,
    Who bids the light of day,

3 With equal radiance to gild
    The simplest shrub or flower,
As the tall cedar that may build
    A temple or a tower.

4 Ye erring multitudes who bow
    To kings of transient date,

> To heaven's Sovereign homage bow,
> Whose will controls your fate.

5 God's majesty and mercy sing,
> All ye, whose pleasant lot
> Is cast where freedom's altars spring,
> And where her creed is taught.

6 But whether ye as bondmen live,
> Or freemen's rights possess,
> Praise to the Lord for ever give,
> And all his statutes bless. P. M.

6. MORNING.

142 Refresh'd by sleep, that sovereign balm,
> Which best can human woes assuage,
> My spirit feels a holy calm,
> And pious thoughts my soul engage.

2 That soul which but the previous hour
> Had in the world of dreams been lost,
> And perch'd on many a thornless flower,
> Which fields of *fancy* only boast,

3 Return'd from its wild pilgrimage,
> Sings first unto the Lord of light,
> A heav'nly bird in mortal cage,
> Preparing for its final flight.

4 Hear it, O thou, eternal God!
> And grant the blessing it may crave,
> Cherish it, while on earth's abode,
> Receive it, when beyond the grave.

5 Too often in this narrow vale,
> Its note is saddened by distress;

But whether joy or grief prevail,
   Thy name it shall for ever bless.

6 And when it struggles to be free,
   What then is its exalted aim?
 To reach that immortality,
   Where angel hosts Thy praise proclaim.
                                   P. M.

7. EVENING.

143 The Lord, a watchful Guardian, reigns
   O'er all created souls;
 His hand the universe sustains,
   His will its course controls.

2 Conception, at its utmost height,
   Can never comprehend
 The glory, majesty, and might,
   That in Omniscience blend.

3 When musing, I at eventide
   The firmament survey,
 Whose golden orbs, celestial Guide,
   Thy wondrous skill display.

4 In silent adoration lost,
   My soul the earth forgets,
 Itself, like that immortal host,
   A star that never sets.

5 How great the mercy, vast the love
   Of Providence divine,
 Who thus created worlds above,
   For man's delight to shine!

6 Oh! ever in their presence bright,
   Devotion stronger grows,
 Ascending to the God of light,
   Of darkness and repose.
                                   P. M.

8 SPRING.

144
Holy and everlasting One!
With joy we hail the vernal sun,
With pride on nature's temple gaze,
Where spring her sweet oblation lays.

2 Firstlings of fragrance there abound,
Blossoms without a blemish found,
Off'rings, the Levite e'en might prize,
For incense worthy of the skies.

3 To strangers now in Palestine,
The rose of Sharon we resign,
Lilies no more, within its light,
Expand to gladden Israel's sight.

4 Holy and everlasting One!
Glory is from Thy people gone;
Yet praises from *their* lips shall gush,
Who seem, like Thy own burning bush,

5 Endued with some mysterious power,
O'er hostile elements to tower;
A human branch by Heav'n illumed,
Through time to flourish unconsumed.

P. M.

9. WINTER.

145
Oh! sad is nature's aspect now,
When summer-birds no longer sing,
And leaves are dying on each bough,
That were but infants in the spring.

2 So perish youth's ambitious hopes,
The foliage of the tree of life,
Till every verdant relic drops,
Amid the storm of worldly strife.

3 But Providence, for ever kind,
   Hath left to man *one evergreen*,
That, when his blooming hours declined,
   On the grave's border might be seen.

4 That gift is faith! the brightest, best,
   That mercy plants in mortal spheres;
Beneath its shade the spirit blest,
   Its farewell from this earth prepares.

P. M.

146. How sad the wintry hours seem,
   When birds are mute and blossoms die,
That in the Summer's brighter beam,
   Sent song and incense to the sky.

2 Will thoughtless man thus meditate,
   And glean not in his walks abroad,
From nature in each varied state,
   Fresh cause for glorifying God?

3 The frost that lies upon the earth
   Is but the shroud of transient death;
And silently for second birth,
   The plants and herbs prepare beneath.

4 The leafless branch has warned the bird
   Of winter's desolating sway;
The voice of instinct has been heard,
   It warbles 'neath a warmer ray.

5 Shepherds their timid flocks secure
   From blasts that would destroy the shorn,
And God, the Pastor of the poor,
   Protects the feeble and forlorn.

6 Author of seasons! teach my mind
   To view, in each vicissitude,
A Providence divine and kind,
   Whose wonders are for e'er renewed.
P. M.

10. PEACE.

147 O Thou! who, as the Great Unknown,
   From pole to pole art glorified,
Whose lavish hand, for every zone,
   Doth gifts appropriate provide—
Of Thee a special blessing now
   Most fervently do we implore,
That discord may no shadow throw
   On freedom's altar evermore.

2 Let thrones of righteous judgment here
   Throughout all future years be found;
And may that spirit disappear,
   Whose breath pollutes her hallowed
      ground,—
That selfish spirit which pursues,
   (Regardless of a neighbor's right,)
Each purpose that promotes its views,
   Or raises it to power's height.

3 Serene, harmonious, and sublime,
   Let peace prevail from age to age,
Untarnished by the stroke of time,
   Or rude assault of jealous rage.
From civil conflict keep us free,
   Abhorrent to the pious mind—
And grant us, Father, peace with Thee,
   With conscience, and with all mankind.
P. M.

148 Is there within the world's wide bound
A place where peace may e'er be found?
Oh! not in palaces of pride
Will Heaven's messenger abide.

2 With glory she will not sojourn,
But from its trophies trembling turn,
Nor long with human love remain,
That born on earth, must bear its stain.

3 She passeth not the gates of sin,
Nor want nor wealth her smile can win;
She droppeth not her olive-leaf
Upon the couch of pain or grief.

4 What being then on mortal ground,
By peace hath ever yet been crowned?
She dwelleth as a seraph guest,
With such as succor the opprest.

5 Her blessing ever is with those
Who freely will forgive their foes,
Who, firm in faith, in feeling pure,
The One Eternal God adore.   P. M.

11. OUR COUNTRY.

149 Father of nations! Judge divine!
    From Thy blessed realms above
Thine ear to prayers and hymns incline,
    Breathed by patriotic love.
Is there one upon this earth,
    Who in welfare or in woe,
For the country of his birth,
    Feels not sympathy's strong glow?

2 Oh! may we not this feeling trace
    To creation's primal date?
When the great parent of our race
    Felt the exile's bitter fate?
His first tears were not for toil,
    But for his lost flower-land—
Paradise, *his* native soil,
    Closed on him by God's command.

3 That pure sentiment was nursed
    When man's innocence had waned;
His progeny, where'er dispersed,
    Kept this virtue unprofaned.
Native to all human kind
    Is the sod of Liberty!
Where no tyrant's law may bind
    Souls by nature's God made free.

4 Brethren! let hearts and voices blend
    In one deep and earnest prayer,
That Heaven's blessings may descend
    Upon Freedom's hallowed sphere;
Where untrammeled faith may sing
    Fearless of the bigot's frown,
But to *One Celestial* King
    Bowing her pure spirit down.

5 Where, upon wisdom's equal plan,
    Conscience no controller dreads,
Secure that on the rights of man
    No usurping despot treads;
Where unto the highest throne,
    Free-will offerings are brought,
Homage to that One alone,
    In whose image we are wrought.

6 Fountain of justice, truth, and peace!
   May these virtues animate,
Until life itself shall cease,
   All the sons of freedom's state.
Grant, that when transferred to earth,
   (As religion's charter shows,)
In heaven, where our souls had birth,
   They at last may find repose.   P. M.

12. PENITENCE.

150 Oh! answer me, my God! this day
   Of abstinence and prayer;
Put my transgressions far away,
   And soften my despair.

2 Answer me, Thou! in whom alone
   A Saviour I behold,
When I confess before Thy throne
   My frailties manifold.

3 But in what language shall I paint
   The depth of my remorse,
For sins of free-will and constraint,
   Done in my evil course?

4 The vast, the awful aggregate,
   My conscious soul confounds;
Pity, O Lord! and meliorate
   Thy servant's moral wounds.

5 Oh! answer me, eternal King!
   When, overwhelmed with shame,
I to Thy sacred altar cling,
   And call upon Thy name.

6 Sinner in practice and in speech,
    Yet dare I hope for grace;
For angel-mercy fills the breach
    Where wrath once found a place.   P. M.

(Partially paraphrased from the 51st Psalm.)

151 Have mercy on Thy servant, Lord!
    According to Thy loving kindness;
And from my spirit ever ward
    That worst of evils—moral blindness.

2 Oft doth the world man's deeds applaud,
    His seeming righteousness believing;
But Thy all-searching eye, O God!
    There is no power of deceiving.

3 This witnesses each guilty thought,
    Watches each criminal impression,
Long, long before it has been wrought
    Into an active, bold transgression.

4 Wisdom that in the inward part,
    With pure truth should in alliance dwell,
Forsakes too oft my feeble heart,
    Prone against Thy statutes to rebel.

5 Oh! wash me with Thy gracious hand,
    Thou whose judgments e'er are justified,
That in Thy presence I may stand,
    From unhallowed passions purified.

6 Thoroughly cleansed by Thee alone
    Can the children of corruption be;
No *hyssop* upon earth is known
    That can from stain the spirit free.

7 Oh! give me, Father, some kind token,
 That Thou wilt change to songs of
  gladness,
 Prayers that from a spirit broken,
  Have been breathed here in contrite
   sadness.

8 With sacrifice Thou wilt dispense,
  Glorious Author of Creation!
 But to the soul that sin repents
  Hast promised pardon and salvation.
                                       P. M.

ISAIAH, CHAP. LVIII.

152 Leaders of Israel, arise!
  Shout with a trumpet-tone,
 The Lord, our God, ne'er sanctifies
  Fasts of the flesh alone.

2 Behold! in strife and loud debate,
  Your sinful lives are spent;
 Falsehood ye freely circulate,
  To nourish discontent.

3 And ye for trespasses like these,
  The flesh would mortify;
 Such sacrifice will ne'er appease
  The Sov'reign of the sky.

4 Thy brother from the yoke release,
  Thy neighbor's burden bear;
 Speak to the widow words of peace,
  The orphan's loss repair.

5 Then glorious as morning light
  Shall ye be seen to shine;
 Such deeds find grace in Heaven's sight,
  And soften wrath divine.   P. M.

153 What painful mem'ries from the buried past
Doth conscience rouse, my soul in gloom to cast!
Her whisper changing to a tone as loud,
As when the thunder rends the summer cloud.

2 Remorse now speaks of sabbath-days profaned,
That some poor gift of fortune might be gained,
Of shrines neglected, by the righteous built,
And perseverance in the path of guilt.

3 God's grace, made manifest by word and sign,
Could not to holiness my heart incline;
The sin of Achan in my spirit strove
Against each token of a Father's love.

4 For wealth I prayed, and labored from my youth,
In search of this I lost the way of truth;
And when bereavement brought me to the dust,
I dared, O God! to say, Thou wert unjust.

5 But now for riches that can ne'er decay,
For precious faith that passeth not away,
For vital godliness that ever shines
More bright than gems, or gold from earthly mines,

6 The heaven of Thy bounty I entreat,
And cast myself before Thy mercy-seat;

Time cannot tarnish, nor can rust corrode,
The treasures garnered in the Lord's
  abode. P. M.

154 Oh! worship not at glory's shrine,
 Nor bow to wealth or pow'r;
False are their gifts, though held divine
 By beings of an hour.

2 They bring not to thy couch of pain
 Balm-drops to ease thy breast;
They take not from thy soul the stain
 That robs thee of thy rest.

3 The work of faith cannot be done,
 When these the spirit move;
They lead thee from the Holy One,
 The God of truth and love.

4 Look well unto thy *soul's estate!*
 It needeth all thy care,
From sin's rank growth to extricate
 The germ God planted there.

5 Oh! then ere vanisheth thy prime,
 Pray to the Lord Supreme,
That righteousness, in future time,
 Past errors may redeem. P. M.

155 Unto Thine altar, King of kings!
Each contrite worshiper now clings,
While self-accusing conscience reads
The record of all past misdeeds,
Imploring grace at ev'ry pause,
For breach of thy great moral laws.

2 Oh! can the tongue, to falsehood prone,
  Send its appeals to Heaven's throne,
  Where truth exalted and refined,
  (Pure essence of a perfect mind,)
  Supreme in holy beauty sits,
  And light ineffable transmits?

3 Can he who justice has abhorred,
  Believe *that* Power will accord
  Pardon to him, who has transgressed
  Statutes, that human wrongs redressed?
  Sternly the upright spirit frowns
  On mortals who o'erleap its bounds.

4 O God! though great my sins may be,
  From stains like these my soul is free.
  Perverseness, arrogance, and pride
  Have oft Thy precepts set aside;
  For evil, both in word and deed,
  Forgiveness doth Thy servant need.

5 But Thou the penitent will raise,
  Who humbly at thy altar prays.
  Stretch out Thy right hand to the meek,
  Sustain the desolate and weak;
  And in the book of mercy write,
  The broken-hearted and contrite.   P. M.

156 Exalted theme of human praise,
  In filial confidence I raise
    To Thee the voice of prayer;
  Burthened with guilt and shame and grief,
  Father in heaven! for relief
    To Thee I still repair.

2 *Thou* seest the shadows of my heart,
　To man it turns its sunny part,
　　Ashamed of passion's storm.
　In Thy compassion I confide,
　O gentle Judge and gracious Guide!
　　My frailties to reform.

3 Meekly will I Thy chastening bear,
　And sackcloth on my spirit wear,
　　For trespass to atone;
　But pity e'er transcends Thine ire,
　When to Thy footstool, Holy Sire!
　　Sin hath for mercy flown.

4 Now let that attribute divine,
　Upon contrition's tear-drops shine,
　　And like a rainbow rest
　On the horizon of my soul,
　Till ev'ry cloud shall from it roll,
　　And leave it pure and blest.　　P. M.

Psalm CI.

157 From my voice shall virtue's praise proceed,
　　Though my heart bears corruption's blot?
　Oft shall I repeat her holy creed,
　　Yet act as though I knew it not?

2 God of mercy! though this moral grace
　　A stranger to my breast hath been,
　Turn not from a penitent Thy face,
　　Who would a better life begin.

3 An humble pilgrim seeks Thy dwelling,
    Virtue to bless and glorify,
No more against her laws rebelling,
    But in their light to live and die.

4 My tent no flatterer shall profane,
    Favor to win by converse bland,
Nor my household sanctuary stain,
    By aught that breaks the Lord's command.

5 Whatsoe'er with duty may conflict,
    Shall ever from my mind be cast,
Which by discipline, severe and strict,
    May excellence attain at last.

6 Ne'er to me in vain shall widows plead,
    Nor helpless children of the dead;
To those in sorrow's dwelling will I speed,
    With portion of my daily bread.

7 By my Father's will, am I not bound
    To share with my poorer brothers
Manna that, gathered upon my ground,
    Out-measures the grain of others?

8 As a house of God shall be my home,
    Where I in innocence will walk,
Nor shall scorners o'er my threshold come,
    Domestic piety to mock.

9 My song to virtue consecrated,
    Revives her image in my soul,
Which to its God now elevated,
    Counsel implores for its control.   P. M.

158 Cast me not from Thy presence, Lord!
　　When at Thy gracious hands
Forgiveness humbly is implored,
　　For breach of Thy commands.

2 Past years like frowning spectres rise,
　　My spirit to upbraid,
Which pleased with folly's enterprise,
　　The task of faith delayed;

3 The task of plucking vicious weeds,
　　And planting in their stead,
Imperishable moral seeds,
　　By godly culture spread.

4 For sins against Thy holy laws,
　　Behold me self-arraigned!
For coldness in religion's cause,
　　For passions unrestrained.

5 Thy frequent gifts with feeble praise
　　Did I for e'er requite;
And murmurs loud presumed to raise
　　At chastisements, though slight.

6 At Heaven's bar I now appear,
　　A culprit before God;
Hearken, O Mercy! to my prayer,
　　Ere justice lifts the rod.

7 Turn not Thy countenance away,
　　When pardon I entreat;
But let the beams of pity play
　　Around Thy judgment seat.　　P. M.

159 Stranger to that pure ambition,
　　Which to godliness aspires,

Man forgetting his high mission,
  Cherisheth but **vain** desires.

2 What is it for which he toileth,
   Rising early, resting late?
  Things that time's strong finger spoileth
   By the great decree of fate.

3 Power, riches, reputation,
   Draw him from the *one true shrine;*
  These receive his adoration,
   Due but to the Lord Divine.

4 Look within the lofty palace:
   What is it we there behold?
  Venal thirst and vengeful malice,
   Dropping gall in cups of gold.

5 Oh! repent of all your errors,
   Ere the light of life departs;
  Wait not until dying terrors
   Wring confession from your hearts.

P. M.

160 Mournfully chant! for our choir accords
   In sadness of soul with Zion's exiles;
  Plaintive their melodies, pensive their
      words,
    Tears of repentence now banishing
      smiles.

2 Who will to Israel comfort impart?
    Who shall his spirit from sorrow release,
  Bind up the wounds of his penitent heart,
    Bring the glad tidings of pardon and
      peace?

3 *Thou*, Thou alone, who o'er Egypt's red
    wave,
  (When the proud tyrant Thy people
    opprest,)
Did'st rise in majesty, Judah to save,
  And redeemed it with Thy covenant
    blest,—

4 *Thou*, Thou alone, O ineffable God!
  Hope to the contrite canst ever dispense;
Though in the pathway of guilt we have
    trod,
  Mercy will plead for the soul that
    repents.   P. M.

161 Woe unto Zion! she is spoiled
    Of all that made her proud;
God's anger hath her beauty foiled,
    And covered with a cloud.

2 She spreadeth forth her feeble hands,
    But none will comfort yield;
She hath transgressed the Lord's
    commands,
    Her refuge once and shield.

3 Her elders sit upon the ground,
    And troubled silence keep;
With sackcloth they are girded—round
    Her ruined shrine they weep.

4 Mothers, to nature's instinct dead,
    Upon their infants prey;
Youth struggles with the hoary head,
    'Neath famine's horrid sway.

5 The conqueror thy Sabbath mocks,
   Oh Salem! in his pride;
The fox upon thy mountain walks,
   Thy foe is magnified.

6 Woe unto us that we have erred!
   For this our hearts despair;
But let compassion now be stirred,
   Turn not from Israel's prayer!   P. M.

162 Oh! plaintive be the touch and tone
   Of instrument and voice;
A shadow on the heart is thrown,
   It cannot now rejoice.

2 We sing of sorrow upon earth,
   When evil passions woke,
And sin, on those of mortal birth,
   Fastened its iron yoke.

3 Behold in tears a captive band
   'Neath Shinar's willows move,
Writhing beneath rebellion's brand,
   Mourning the land they love.

4 Wisely did we the warning take,
   And from their guilt abstain:
O God! Thy statutes still we break,
   Still slaves to sin remain.

5 Yet blest are we who, tho' afar
   From Zion's sacred fold,
Have found a shrine 'neath freedom's star,
   Where faith is uncontrolled.

6 Oh! hither bring those pearls of price
   Which Mercy will accept,—

Contrition's purest sacrifice,
　　Tears for transgression wept.　　　P. M.

163 Creator of the universe!
When I before Thee would rehearse
　　The trespasses of years,—
Standing on judgment's awful brink,
In terror from the task I shrink,
　　Oppressed by rising fears.

2 Thy consecrated festivals
To me have been no solemn calls
　　To penitence and prayer,
Deserted was Thy dwelling-place,
Unheeded all Thy acts of grace
　　And providential care.

3 Traitor to holiness, I strove
Its force and beauty to disprove,
　　Its excellence to doubt;
No loveliness in faith I saw,
Nor felt that spiritual awe
　　Which fills the soul devout.

4 Thus have I lived unsanctified,
The slave of prejudice and pride,
　　The foe of sacred truth,—
List'ning to pleasure's serpent hiss,
Who, with a bribe of worldly bliss,
　　Beguiled me from my youth.

5 Roused by the cornet's warning blast,
I looked upon the vanished past,
　　And wept for wasted years;
But thou wilt ope compassion's gate,
And all my guilt obliterate,
　　God of supernal spheres!　　　P. M.

VI. SABBATH HYMNS.

164 Gather and worship! The first star of eve
To usher the Sabbath in glory appears,
As that day of rest comes from gloom to
relieve
The spirits that toil in the valley of
tears.

2. Gather and worship! Can Judah forget
The soul-cheering promise of Mercy
supreme?
Though few, where the righteous in God's
name are met,
On these shall the light of His countenance beam.

3 Gather and worship! These hours serene
To labors of holiness e'er dedicate;
With waters of penitence make your
hearts clean,
Or meekly the woes of the poor mitigate.

4 Gather and worship! The stars as they
move,
To faith, in their orbits of glory appear
Like Sabbath-lamps, lighted by angels
above,
To lure human hearts to their own
house of prayer.

5 Gather and worship! The power of time
Shall cause every planet in heaven to
wane;

    But *there*, ever fixed, is a star more
        sublime,
      The soul that on earth has contracted
        no stain.   P. M.

165 Daughters of Israel, arise!
        The Sabbath-morn to greet,
    Send songs and praises to the skies,
        Than frankincense more sweet.

2 Take heed, lest ye the drift mistake
      Of Heaven's hallowed hours,
    And from those dreams too late awake,
      That show you but life's flowers.

3 Leave not the spirit unarrayed,
      To deck the mortal frame;
    With gems of grace let woman aid
      Charms, that from nature came.

4 With jewels of a gentle mind,
      More precious far than gold,
    Brightened by love, by faith refined,
      And set in chastest mould.

5 Wife! mother! sister! on ye all
      A tender task devolves;
    Child, husband, brother, on ye call
      To nerve their best resolves.

6 Your hands must gird the buckler on,
      The moral weapons cleanse,
    By which that battle may be won,
      That in self-conquest ends.   P. M.

166 It is the solemn Sabbath-day,
        Let praise to God ascend;

    In holiness thy soul array,
        And worldly thoughts suspend.

2. Come forth, ye weary sons of care,
        Toil-worn and grief-opprest,
    To heaven send a grateful pray'r,
        For these calm hours of rest.

3. Let not the poorest of ye ask
        Of Providence, (**long** tried,)
    "If I forego my daily task,
        Whose hand will bread provide?"

4. Remember *that* celestial food
        To Israel ordained,
    When **Mercy** *double* portions strewed,
        Lest **Sabbath** be profaned.

5. With ten-fold gifts will God repay
        The transient loss incurred;
    But tremble ye! who disobey
        The mandate of the Lord.   P. M.

167 He spoke—and thro' the gloom profound
        Effulgent light its glory shed;
    He breathed—and all the earth around
        With living myriads soon was spread.

2. How vast, how *holy* was the love,
        That blest us with these gifts divine,
    While angels, in the choir above,
        Sung praises round His heavenly shrine.

3. Nature in primal beauty glow'd,
        Her incense, too, to heaven ascending;
    On every side rich blessings flow'd,
        His mercy with His goodness blending.

4 Still o'er these works of grandeur rose
    A radiant beam—a heavenly ray—
The holy rest, the calm repose,
    That sanctified the Sabbath-day

5 In sacred song our voices swelling,
    Let hallelujahs peal around,
While seraphs, near His starry dwelling
    Shall echo back the grateful sound.
C. M. C.

168 Source of mercy, truth and grace!
    Humbly we this Sabbath-day,
In Thy holy dwelling-place,
    Grateful adoration pay

2 Ere these hours of rest depart,
    Man! recall each past misdeed.
This will purify thy heart,
    And extract corruption's seed.

3 Self-exalted dost thou stand,
    Whilst thy *neighbor* is decried?
Listen to the Lord's command,
    Love shall supersede thy pride.

4 Hast thou dared the *poor* to spurn,
    Though with every virtue graced?
With confusion shalt thou learn,
    These are far *above* thee placed.

5 Is the guilt of *slander* thine?
    Thou wilt shudder at thy wrong,
When thou hearest wrath divine
    Hath denounced its serpent-tongue.

6 Let the *hypocrite* reflect,
    That a spirit-searching God,

      Will his evil ways detect,
         And avenge with penal rod.

7 For this pure and noble end
    Was the Sabbath set apart:
May the Lord of life extend
    Peace to each repentant heart!   P. M.

169 With joyful heart I greet again
      This holy day of rest,
To chant within the sacred fane,
    And bow at Thy behest.

2 On Thee, O God! my hopes rely,
    Thy name be ever praised,
Vouchsafe to bless and sanctify
    These strains devoutly raised.

3 Oh! banish hence, far from my mind,
    All evil thoughts away,
And grant my soul may favor find
    On this, Thy holy day

4 And at the altar as I bend,
    To supplicate Thy care,
In mercy, Lord! Thy blessing send
    Upon my humble prayer.   G. L.

170 God of the Sabbath! to Thy praise,
As once in Zion's palmy days,
    The organ sweetly swells;
While thousands to Thy temples throng,
And in alternate prayer and song,
    Send up their meek appeals.

2 Gently we lay our burdens down,
　Where faith assumes her Sabbath-crown.
　　And wears the robe of peace;
　When from the web of worldly strife,
　We draw that golden thread of life,
　　The seventh day's release.

3 But think not 'tis enough, that we
　Our hands from servile labor free
　　On this most holy day:
　If malice in the soul still works,
　If *there* one spark of anger lurks,
　　In vain we sing and pray.

4 When shall the jubilee begin,
　That from the slavery of sin,
　　Man's spirit shall redeem?
　Not till we plant with pious toil,
　On Sabbaths, in the moral soil,
　　The law of God supreme.　　　　P. M.

171 In harmony with Heaven's peace,
　　Sabbath's deep repose descends,
　From toil the weary to release,
　　The sordid draw from worldly ends
　Lord! let devotion fill our hearts,
　Ere time's serenest day departs.

2 Rest, worshipers! and pray and sing,
　　To the Healer of all woes,
　From whose exhaustless, balmy spring
　　Consolation ever flows.
　Here will the burthened spirit gain
　Courage, all trials to sustain.

3 Thine, Father! is the mighty will,
　　And Thine the gracious pow'r,

The tumults of the mind to still,
   In sorrow's stormy hour.
Nor e'er unsolaced shall they grieve,
Who righteously Thy word receive.

4 O God! let passion's flood recede
   From Thy hallowed dwelling-place,
Lest from the soul Thy moral creed
   Its wild current may efface:
And from that *inner temple* sweep
The statutes we should therein keep.

5 Hear us! when we uplift our hands
   In fervent supplication,
That Thou wilt bless and speed all plans
   For freedom's preservation,
And o'er the country of our love,
Let peace, the Sabbath-angel, move.

6 Come, ye afflicted and forlorn!
   To this consecrated shrine,
Where e'en the breast by anguish torn
   Care forgets in rest divine—
In the fullness of devotion,
Merging every sad emotion.   P. M.

172 Now let the hand of toil suspend
      Its daily task severe,
   And youth and age their voices blend,
      In glad and grateful prayer.

2 Behold! the Sabbath sun appears
      Beneficient and bright,
   As if it drew from higher spheres
      A part of Mercy's light!

3 Pause ye, whom sordid schemes engross
    In virtue's balance weighed,
  Your present gain is future loss,
    Your substance but a shade.

4 And ye, whom pleasure can beguile,
    From piety to stray,
  Pause! and 'gainst her hollow smile,
    God's awful frown array.

5 Come hither, ye by sorrow bowed!
    For pure and earnest prayer
  Hath power to dispel each cloud.
    Of mortal grief and care.

6 The mourner's failing hope revives,
    Beneath that sacred dome,
  Where faith divine a promise gives,
    Of Sabbaths yet to come.   Г. М.

173 Praise the Lord God, the glorious
      Supreme!
  Whose Sabbath we the highest gift esteem,
  By His munificence on man bestowed,
  Since first on earth the fount of mercy
      flowed.

2 Praise the ineffable, eternal One!
  Whose holy will with rev'rence should be
      done,
  Who to angelic hosts proclaimed on high,
  This day for ever shall ye sanctify!

3 O crowning evidence of love and grace!
  O best of blessings to the human race!
  Shall we thy lustre dim by deeds impure,
  Seeking some worldly treasure to secure.

4 Let it not be! Let feeling, thought, and word,
   With this day's sweet serenity accord;
   In vain the hand its daily task foregoes,
   If the *mind* labors and rejects repose.

5 There is a soil *within* that culture needs—
   A moral field o'errun with evil weeds—
   These to extract, this holy time employ,
   Lest they the growth of righteousness destroy.

6 Be this, O Israel! your sacred task,
   And not in vain shall ye God's blessing ask;
   Sing hallelujahs, children of His choice,
   And in the Sabbath of the Lord rejoice.

                                            P. M.

EZEKIEL, XX., v. 20.

174 Hallow my Sabbaths! Will Israel respond,
    With filial delight, to his Father's command?
      Or sever by trespass the holiest bond
        That ever was signed by His merciful hand?

  2 Hallow my Sabbaths! Elect of all nations,
      The voice of the prophet is lifted in *vain;*
        Earth taketh from heaven your vows and oblations,
          Your prayer is for *power*—your precept is *gain.*

3 Hallow my Sabbaths! Can Jeshurun
    falter,
  When God for a *single day's sacrifice*
    pleads?
Void is the temple, and vacant the altar,
  The world's profane service His worship
    impedes.

4 Hallow my Sabbaths! The hand of life's
    dial
  Moves rapidly on, in its limited sphere,
While faith keeps her eye on that hour of
    trial,
  When man must his soul to Omnipotence
    bear.

5 Hallow my Sabbaths! By this ye shall
    merit,
  With angels in bright convocation to
    meet,
The kingdom of Heaven for e'er to inherit,
  And sing with the saints before God's
    mercy-seat.   P. M.

175 Prepare and purify my heart,
    Thou who receivest mortal prayer!
  Its Sabbath-thoughts to set apart
    From every worldly hope and fear.

2 Oh! lead my spirit far away,
    From evil haunts of human-kind;
  Withdraw it from the fragile clay,
    In which Thou hast its light enshrined.

3 Let not Thy servant pass unblest,
    From mercy's hallowed dwelling-place;

There, when my frailties are confest,
   Give me assurance of Thy grace. P. M.

176 Rest for the Lord ! The work is done,
   That order out of chaos brought,
Gave to the firmament a sun,
   To man—the glorious light of *thought*.

2 Rest for the new-created globe !
   Forth went the law of love divine,
And peace put on her purest robe,
   And smiling stood at Eden's shrine.

3 Brighter the flower-altar grew,
   As there the Sabbath-angel prayed,
That her own spirit might imbue
   All that by Mercy had been made.

4 But when serenity departs,
   And sin has closed its golden gate ;
When thorns spring up in human hearts,
   And tears reveal man's altered state :

5 Most sensibly will sons of earth,
   (Of costly knowledge once possest,)
Appreciate the real worth
   Of hallowed periodic rest.

6 O ye ! whose paradise is found,
   Not where the leaves of truth expand,
But where the fruits of wealth abound,
   Remember Heaven's great command.

7 Six days to labor ye may give,
   But on the seventh shall repose,
That in the land ye long may live,
   Which with God's bounty overflows.

8 Fulfilled—ye shall in spheres above,
   (Where centuries like hours roll,)
Enjoy the gift of perfect love—
   Th' eternal Sabbath of the soul.   P. M.

177 Praise to the God of nations sing,
   Who in sublime repose,
Bade Sabbath into being spring,
   Creation's work to close.

2 The solace which this day of rest
   To suff'ring mortals brings,
Must take from ev'ry troubled breast
   The sharpest of its stings.

3 Banished from Eden, and bereaved
   By guilt of all its flow'rs,
Oh! how would toiling man have grieved,
   But for these hallowed hours.

4 Yet, oh! beware, lest sin once more
   In God's own temple creep,
And tempt thy spirit as before,
   When faith was lulled to sleep.

5 Though now the proffered fruit be gold,
   Turn from the gift away,—
For this, immortal souls are sold
   On Heaven's holy day.

6 Upon thy conscience leave no stain,
   So durable and deep,
As that of giving up to *gain*
   The Sabbath angels keep.   P. M.

VII. FESTIVAL HYMNS.

1. NEW YEAR.

178 Between the past and future year,
We pause awhile in our career,
   Two voices to attend;
One speaks of life, and light, and bloom,
One warns us of the unseen tomb,
   To which all must descend.

2 *Experience and hope* thus stand,
Addressing all the human band,
   As on they swiftly speed;
Young pilgrims but the promise hear,
That time in every coming year
   Will but to pleasure lead.

3 Few, even of maturest age,
Can that grave wisdom long engage,
   Which for reflection calls;
Still blind and rash, they forward pass,
The last few minutes of their glass
   Wasting in mirth's gay halls.

4 Oh! listen to the warning tone,
In sorrow sent from mem'ry's throne,
   Ye children of the dust!
No falsehood rests upon the tongue,
That counsels both the old and young,
   In God alone to trust.

5 Oh! what a crowd of by-gone things,
Home to the heart remembrance brings,
   At our annual feast;

Many with smiles their kindred greet,
Some weeping, show each vacant seat
   Once filled by friends deceased.

6 Look round on nature's varied scene,
What chequered objects lie between
   The cradle and the bier—
The sunbeam and the stormy cloud,
The wedding-raiment and the shroud
   Sadden, by turns, and cheer.

7 Now on that *inner being* gaze,
Where passion oft its shadow lays
   On all that once was bright;
Where pride so frequently expels
That love in which God's likeness dwells,
   Reflecting moral light.

8 Remember that a day, an hour,
May place beyond all mortal pow'r
   Forgiveness to bestow;
Let not the New Year's sun decline,
Ere ye have vowed before this shrine
   Resentment to forego.

9 Put off each ling'ring weakness now,
Faith will your minds with strength endow,
   Self-conquest to achieve;—
Will give you fortitude to bear
The chastenings, frequent and severe,
   Ye may on earth receive.

10 Oh! then shall Mercy's hand record
That blessed, that benignant word:
   Pardon to sinful man!
Whose soul, triumphant o'er decay,
To *that* world shall direct its way,
   Which knows no annual span.   P. M.

179 Into the tomb of ages past
Another year hath now been cast
Shall time, unheeded, take its flight,
Nor leave one ray of moral light,
That on man's pilgrimage may shine,
And lead his soul to spheres divine?

2 Ah! which of us, if self-reviewed,
Can boast unfailing rectitude?
Who can declare his wayward will
More prone to righteous deeds than ill?
Or, in his retrospect of life,
No traces find of passion's strife?

3 A "still small voice," as time departs,
Bids us inspect our secret hearts,
Whose hidden depths too oft contain
Some *spot*, which suffered to remain,
Will (slight at first) by sad neglect
The hue of *vice* at last reflect.

4 With firm resolve your bosoms nerve
The God of truth alone to serve,
Speech, thought, and act to regulate,
By what His perfect laws dictate;
Nor from His sanctuary stray,
By worldly idols lured away.

5 Peace to the house of Israel!
May joy within it ever dwell!
May sorrow on the opening year,
Forgetting its accustomed tear,
With smiles again fond kindred meet,
With hopes revived the festal greet!

P. M.

180 Morn breaks upon Moriah's height:
A father and his only son

There bow towards the rising light,
   And humbly say, God's will be done!

2 With trembling hand but faithful heart,
   The sire binds his sinless boy,
Prepared with that sweet pledge to part,
   Which he who lent would now destroy.

3 On Sarah most his thoughts were bent,
   When she no more should meet her child;
But mourn within her lonely tent
   For him, the pure, the undefiled.

4 Yet firmly Abram grasps the blade:
   But e'er the fatal stroke descends,
A beam hath round the victim played,
   An angel o'er the altar bends.

5 Forbear! the test of faith is o'er!
   Unbind the sacrificial cord!
Yon Heav'n provided ram secure,
   To bleed and burn before the Lord.

6 Blow, blow the trumpet of gladness now!
   God's clemency and love confess!
Who hath fulfilled His solemn vow,
   In Isaac's seed the earth to bless.

P. M.

181 Look down, O God! with gracious eye
   On Thy worshipers contrite!
And let each penitential sigh,
   Thy compassion now excite.
When we Thy sanctuary seek,
In solemn prayer, with spirit meek,
   Past transgressions to declare,

No judge relentless wilt Thou prove,
But with a father's boundless love,
   Pardon grant on this New Year.

2 Look down in mercy, mighty King!
   Upon our domestic spheres—
Remove from these whate'er may bring
   Remorse in our future years.
From our beloved home-circles keep
The shadows dark and sorrows deep,
   Encountered in life's career.
Banish from there all passions stern,
And to the course of virtue turn
   Our hearts on this New Year.

3 Look down upon this city, Lord!
   And all danger and distress
From its remotest limits ward,
   With parental tenderness.
Increase, kind Providence! the store
Of the honest, laboring poor,
   Who in mind Thy statutes bear;
Relieve the sons of want and woe,
That tears may not be seen to flow
   On the birth of this New Year.

4 Look down and bless, eternal King!
   Thy holy habitation,
Where sinners to Thy altar cling,
   In contrite supplication.
Not for ourselves alone we pray—
For fellow-creatures gone astray
   We implore forgiveness *here!*
O God! when we depart from hence,
In heaven may our soul commence
   Immortality's New Year.   P. M.

2. DAY OF ATONEMENT.

182
My heart is bared to Thee, O Lord!
   Rebellious oft against Thy laws;
My frailties *justice* must record,
   But, oh! let *mercy* plead my cause.

2 That angel finds a saving grace,
   Where sterner truth but guilt descries:
Her shrine is still a shelt'ring place,
   To which the trembling sinner flies.

3 To other gods I've gone astray,
   Idols of man's own fabrication,
Riches and fame, that flee away,
   And leave the soul in desolation.

4 I've dwelt with unrelenting stress,
   Upon my neighbor's lightest sin,
And looked with partial tenderness
   Upon the deeper taint within.

5 Proud, covetous, vindictive, vain,
   Thy contrite servant oft hath been;
Yet from Thy chast'ning rod refrain,
   O God! and let me pardon win.

6 Thus have I rent the flimsy veil,
   That hid my heart's deformity,
Not yet beyond salvation's pale,
   If mercy will but plead for me.   P. M.

183
Lord of the world! when I behold
   The ling'ring shadows of the night,
Far, far from the horizon rolled,
   By the effulgent source of light—

2 Cheered is my soul, howe'er oppressed;
    For thus it trusts will mercy's ray
Shine on the penitential breast,
    And chase the clouds of sin away.

3 Yet, while my eye from nature takes
    A token that may hope convey,
A secret dread my spirit shakes,
    O God! upon this fearful day.

4 The mourner's dust should strew my head,
    The shroud my fitting raiment prove;
For now my sentence must be read
    By the eternal Judge above.

5 Woe, woe is me! the vain, the proud,
    The votary of idle mirth;
E'en as a bulrush am I bowed,
    By conscious frailty to the earth.

6 Peace, mortal man! nor in despair
    Forget there is a mighty Hand,
Which can redemption's standard rear,
    And break corruption's iron band.

7 But, oh! if thou wouldst grace entreat
    Of Him who rends the yoke of sin,
That mercy let thy brother meet,
    Which thou wouldst from thy Father win.

8 The wicked Thou wilt not forsake,
    Almighty Sovereign and Sire!
But from their hearts defilement shake,
    And love of purity inspire.

9 Shepherd of Israel! Thy rod
    Hath driven us from Zion's fold;
Let us, through righteousness, O God!
    The better land of faith behold.   P. M.

184 Eternal love is Thine, O God!
　Oh! let me not in error stray,
But chasten with a gentle rod,
　And lead me back to virtue's way.

2 With penitential tears I weep,
　Turn not away, in wrath, Thy face;
Awake my soul from sinful sleep,
　And purify it by Thy grace.

3 Thou, who canst heal the broken heart,
　Will hear the suppliant's prayer;
Thy truth, Thy goodness, oh! impart:
　Almighty, take me to Thy care!

C. D. L. H.

185 Father of mercies! on this morning,
　Trembling I stand before Thy shrine,
Appalled by conscience, whose fore-
　　warning
　Sternly prefigures wrath divine,
Whose bolt, (forgiving as Thou art,)
Hath stricken oft the sinful heart.

2 Yet, though opprest with shame and
　　terror,
　Freely will I to Thee expose
Each foible and each flagrant error,
　That from unbridled passion grows,
Though from Omniscience none may
　　screen
Guilt, that no mortal eye hath seen.

3 But, O my Judge and Benefactor!
　What trespass shall be first proclaimed?
The slander of the base detractor,
　Whose shaft at *more* than life is aimed,

  That e'er with jealousy conspires,
  To mar what all the world admires?

4 Or, from my manifold offences,
  Shall I that scornful pride select,
 Which all its love in *self* condenses,
  And will no social tie respect,
 Frustrating thus Thy gracious end,
 In fellowship mankind to blend?

5 Eternal Sovereign! Sire supreme!
  When I Thy glory should promote,
 My powers to some worldly scheme
  Unrighteously do I devote,
 And e'en Thy Sabbaths oft profane,
 Some selfish object to attain.

6 Alas! were all these faults forgiven,
  So many would remain untold,
 That to despair I should be driven,
  Did I not in remembrance hold
 Thy mercy, from creation's birth,
 Dispensed to sinners upon earth.

7 Oh! may that shield of the offender,
  On this great judgment-day arise,
 And prompt Thee, Father! to surrender
  The scourge, uplifted to chastise!
 Thy boundless grace for me shall ope
 The gates of pardon, peace, and hope.

P. M.

186
Comfort ye, O Israel! and lift no more
   The voice of trembling and of tribu-
      lation;
  But songs of gladness and thanksgiving
      pour
   To Him who hears and answers
      supplication.

2 Comfort ye, frail transgressors! Hence
      depart,
   Cheered by the belief that He who
      reigns above,
  Will to himself draw every contrite heart
   With the soft chords of pure, paternal
      love.

3 But ere ye from this holy place retreat,
   Vow, *firmly* vow, before the throne of
      Heaven,
  That ye will never more those sins repeat
   Which God, in mercy, hath this day
      forgiven.

4 Turn to your home! But, oh! remember
      there
   The pious purposes *here* meditated!
  Let each man's dwelling be a house of
      prayer,
   To peace, to love, to justice consecrated.

                                    P. M.

3. TABERNACLES.

187 How desolate thy fields and vales,
    O Palestine! once fair and free—
No reaper-train the harvest hails
    With hymns to Israel's Deity.

2 The torch hath been upon thy sheaf,
    The brand upon thy fruitful vine,
And thou art like a withered leaf,
    Hurled to the dust by wrath divine.

3 No more upon thy blighted soil
    The tents of all the tribes arise;
Thou art indeed a prey and spoil—
    Thy crown and sceptre Ishmael's prize.

4 Afar we tabernacles rear,
    And seek a righteous substitute,
In grateful praise and godly prayer,
    For offerings of grain and fruit.

5 Myrtles and willows we entwine,
    And palm and fairer citron bring,
Creations of *one* Hand divine,
    From which all nature's blessings
        spring.

6 And as we thus together place
    Inodorous and fragrant boughs,
So mingle, too, the human race,
    Whom God with diverse gifts endows.

7 Our habitations we forsake
    For booths, whose open roofs reveal
That heaven, to whose Lord we make
    Our first address and last appeal.

8 Such change the pious soul prepares
   For final passage to the grave,
Whence it may reach immortal spheres,
   Where saints the palm of glory wave!

9 O Thou! whose presence glorified
   Our pilgrim fathers' desert-tents,
Let truth be now our angel-guide,
   And light to Israel dispense!   P. M.

188 Praise the Counselor supreme!
   Oh! praise the Judge divine!
Who deigned Judah to redeem,
   With wonder, word, and sign.
Feeble must all language prove,
   His glories to rehearse,
Tokens of whose boundless love
   Make glad the universe.

2 Led from Egypt's servile sod,
   Our sires (a pilgrim band)
Trackless wilds securely trod
   To Canaan's vine-clad land.
Frail the tent, but firm the trust,
   Of Israel that day;
For, through desert-clouds of dust,
   He still saw Mercy's ray.

3 Lost to us is that blessed soil
   Whose trees shed fragrant tears;
But the Hand that wrought the spoil,
   Fresh drops of balm prepares.
Genial now, as in the past,
   Are beam, and breeze, and dew,
Which, for toiling man's repast,
   The harvest-fruits renew

4 *Now*, on freedom's rock sublime,
    God's moral law is read;
  Now, as in the elder time,
    The wilderness yields bread.
  Set your tabernacles up,
    Ye righteous Hebrews! here,
  Sanctify your sweetened cup
    With sacred song and prayer.

5 In life's wilderness, man's fame
    A transient booth appears,
  Where the soul, that from God came,
    Dwells for a few brief years.
  Lord! when from this fabric slight
    My spirit shall remove,
  Guide it *Thou* to heaven's height.
    The promised land of love!   P. M.

189 Rude are the tabernacles now
       Of Israel's scattered band;
     Still to the East the faithful bow,
       And bless their fatherland.
     Oh! save us, we beseech Thee, Lord!
     Through every chance and change
             adored

  2 Oh! when we think of Palestine.
       Whose consecrated dust
    Once bore the hallowed ark and shrine
       Of Judah's only Trust:
    We mourn to mark the stranger there,
    Who only mocks the Hebrew's prayer.

  3 Wake ye, who in the deadly sleep
       Of self-delusion lie!

    Arise! or ye may live to weep
       The time now passing by.
    Save us, O everlasting Lord!
    Thy aid against remorse afford.

 4 Let us re-open mercy's law,
       And in our bosoms lock
    Precepts, that humble hearts shall draw
       Towards salvation's rock;
    Praises to heaven's supreme Lord,
    Who did this sovereign gift accord!

                                    P. M.

190 Of Heaven's bounties let us sing,
       That, countless as the stars above,
    Through all the varied seasons spring
       From the eternal Source of love!
    Mirrored alike on vale and mount,
       Are images of Grace benign;
    Fields, moistened o'er by Mercy's fount,
       To yield the reaper wheat and wine.

 2 In spring, the whisp'ring breezes give
       God's gracious message to the earth,
    That languid nature shall revive,
       And all that's beautiful have birth.
    Brief the life-time of the flowers;
       But scarcely have these passed away,
    When the autumnal harvest-hours
       Come to atone for their decay.

 3 Shall lab'ring man on fallen leaves
       Bestow his unavailing tears,
    When on their ruin rise the sheaves
       Whose golden grain his spirit cheers?

No! joyously he then should lift
   His grateful heart to God in prayer,
Who to the season suits the gift,
   But ne'er suspends a parent's care.

4 With moral providence, likewise,
   Let beings of this world prepare
'Gainst days when youth's bright verdure
      dies,
   And life is like the waning year.
For then shall virtue vegetate,
   And flourish on the *inner ground*;
Joy shall the reaper animate,
   Within whose tents its fruits are found.

P. M.

191 How great, how pure is my delight,
   Thee to serve and praise, O Lord!
Thy wondrous judgements to recite,
   Thy kind precepts to record.
Let my career be sanctified
   From *this* day by godly deeds,
And through *that* path my footsteps guide
   Which to thy own kingdom leads.

2 With *spiritual manna*, Thou
   Craving hearts hast e'er sustained:—
Nourish with two-fold portion now
   Those whose moral strength was waned.
Again, again, O gracious King!
   By Thy mild, paternal grace
Am I allowed to pray and sing
   In Thy blessed dwelling-place.

3 Oh! that my thoughts were like my
     theme,
　Holy, glorious, and pure;
 That they would with reflected beam,
　Come *from* Thee and *to* Thee soar!
 Alas! but *half* immortal here,
　The soul no power can boast,
 Of sending on the wings of prayer,
　Thoughts that glorify Thee most.

4 Yet even prayer from lips defiled,
　With indulgence have been heard—
 On the suppliant Thou hast smiled,
　Who with tears his plea preferred.
 Me Thou never hast rejected,
　When towards Thy mercy-seat
 ·Faith my spirit hath directed,
　Thy forgiveness to entreat.

5 With what can we compare the joy,
　Lord! of tending at Thy shrine,
 The rapture, free from all alloy,
　Of a service so divine?
 Oh! grant our lives through future years
　One long festival may prove,
 And we from seeds first sown in tears,
　Fruits may reap of peace and love.

P. M.

4. FEAST OF DEDICATION.

192 Great Arbiter of human fate,
　Whose glory ne'er decays,
 To Thee alone we dedicate
　The song and soul of praise.

2 Thy presence Judah's host inspired,
    On danger's post to rush;
By Thee the Maccabee was fired,
    Idolatry to crush.

3 Amid the ruins of their land,
    (In Salem's sad decline,)
Stood forth a brave but scanty band
    To battle for their shrine.

4 In bitterness of soul they wept,
    Without the temple wall;
For weeds around its courts had crept,
    And foes its priests enthral.

5 Not long to vain regrets they yield,
    But for their cherished fane,
Nerved by true faith they take the field,
    And victory obtain.

6 But whose the power, whose the hand,
    Which thus to triumph led
That slender but heroic band,
    From which blasphemers fled?

7 'Twas Thine, O everlasting King
    And universal Lord!
Whose wonder still thy servants sing,
    Whose mercies they record.

8 The priest of God his robe resumed,
    When Israel's warlike guide
The sanctuary's lamp relumed,
    Its altar purified.

9 Oh! thus shall Mercy's hand delight
    To cleanse the blemished heart,
Rekindle virtue's waning light,
    And peace and truth impart.   P. M.

193 God dwells in light!
His first commanding word on earth,
Which at creation's glorious birth
Resounded, was: "Let there be light!"
    The sun-lit beam
    His tender stream,
Of love a symbol clear and bright.

2   God dwells in light!
Upon the lucid paths of life,
Redeemed from error, inward strife,
Let us proceed by wisdom led;
    In happiness
    And in distress,
The light of God be on us shed!

3   God dwells in light!
A holy, heav'nly spark in trust
He gave to ev'ry child of dust,
Prepared by Him, th' Eternal One;
    A brilliant ray
    To shine by day,
But not to set when life is gone.

4   God dwells in light!
He broke the sinner's mighty hand,
And crushed the despot's haughty band,
In glorious days of olden time;
    And ne'er to wane
    In Israel's fane
Rekindled was His light sublime.

5   God dwells in light!
In Him, oh! let us now rejoice,
And raise to him the heart and voice,
Who worketh wonders evermore;

　　　　　The guiltless tear
　　　　　With light to cheer,
　　He changeth not, our God of yore!

6　　　　God dwells in light!
　　He touched the champions' pious hearts
　　With fire, that courage e'er imparts,
　　For faith above all time and space!
　　　　　Guard truth and love,
　　　　　Sent from above—
　　Thou'lt triumph then, God's priestly race!
　　　　　　　　　　　　　　M. M.

194 Arise! let the souls of the Hebrews rejoice,
　　As they glorify God with the heart and the voice,
　　Who with power sublime the oppressor did crush,
　　As *He* led the bold Maccabee onward to rush.

2 When idolatry darkened that beautiful land,
　　Thy spirit inspired and nerved a brave band,—
　　Nor long did the cloud their loved temple surround,
　　For a mighty Hand Judah with victory crowned.

3 Then th' altar so sullied by blasphemy's breath,
　　Became holy and pure 'neath the conqueror's wreath;

And the nations of God clung around the
    lov'd shrine,
From their foes thus released by Thy
    mercy divine.

4 How bright o'er her ruins shone Salem's
    lone star,
As the Maccabee proudly came forth from
    the war!
And from many brave hearts did thanks-
    giving ascend,
As they gathered before their own altar
    to bend.

5 Great God of the faithful! unto Thee,
    Thee alone,
Must we bow in submission before Thy
    great throne;
For Thou, O Creator! in Thy mercy wilt
    save
And redeem ev'ry soul from the gloom of
    the grave.   C. M. C.

5. FEAST OF ESTHER.

195 Almighty God! Thy special grace,
    In seasons of distress,
Hath ever, by the Hebrew race,
    Been gratefully confest.

2 When lots were cast, with evil aim,
    Thy people to destroy,
From Thee the great decision came
    That turned their tears to joy.

3 Earth's mightiest, at Thy decree,
   E'en to the frailest yield,
And Susa's shore and Egypt's sea
   Proclaim Thee Israel's Shield.

4 The mourner at the palace-gate,
   The maiden on the throne
Were but the instruments of fate
   To make God's mercy known.

5 To Thee alone the praise belongs,
   Who, with a father's hand,
From Judah's race averts the wrongs
   By adversaries planned.

6 Let proud, ungodly men, elate
   With triumphs of an hour,
Remember, heaven can frustrate
   Each dark device of pow'r.

7 Sov'reign of worlds! *Thou* wilt extend
   Thy sceptre to the just,
The rights of innocence defend,
   And bring its foes to dust.   **P. M.**

196 O God! To-day our joyful song of praise,
   Which grateful love and piety attune,
Unto Thy glorious throne on high we raise,
   While here with Thee devoutly we commune.

2 Thou scornest falsehood, hatest vengeful plans,
   And penetratest all malignant hearts;
Thine all-pervading eye the spirit scans,
   That from religion's holy law departs.

3 Pure innocence, by guilt and crime
  oppressed,
 Must often weep, by Thee unheeded long;
 While *these* with fortune's rev'ling joys
  are blessed,
 Affliction, pain, and grief round *that* will
  throng.

4 But **when, at last,** the sinner's cup
  o'erflows,
 Thou wilt, **O God! Thy** justice yet
  reveal,
The deep-laid schemes of crime it **over-
  throws**,
 To punish guilt, and innocence to heal.

5 Sublime reward of bliss, thine all-just hand
 Will on long-suffering piety bestow,
And virtue's brilliant crown and golden
  band
 Will then adorn **her** calm and cheerful
  brow.   M. M.

6. PASSOVER.

197 God of the earth, **the air, the** sea,
 Source of Israel's salvation!
Whose power set our fathers **free**
 From Egypt's task and tribulation;
Through ages **shall** their seed proclaim
Their glorious Redeemer's **name**.

2 Thy angel in the pillar stood,
 Towering, by turns, in flame and cloud,

And bade the *winds* pass o'er the flood,
    To shield the meek and blast the proud;
The song of Miriam evermore
Shall echo find from freedom's shore.

3 Here every bosom holds a chord,
    That to her grateful strain **responds**,
Ascribing glory to the **Lord**,
    Who can alone break human bonds.
Praise to the Guide of Israel's host,
Who maketh vain the **tyrant's boast**.

4 Let every soul be purified
    From dark *corruption's* fatal *leaven*,
Nor in its blind and *stubborn* pride,
    Reject the **manna sent** from heaven—
The pure, sweet seed of revelation,
By Mercy dropt for man's salvation.   P. M.

198

Oh! let us mingle heart and **voice**,
In unison let us rejoice,
    To one **great** God appealing;
The children of the Hebrew race,
Who, tho' divided now by space,
    Are linked by fate and feeling.
        Bondage **hath ceased**,
        And freedom's feast
        For souls released,
        By mem'ry kept,
        Each chord hath swept,
In which **her** sacred music slept.

2 The sword of vengeance flashed abroad!
    The sceptre that became a *rod*
        Has by a rod been broken;

The child redeemed from Nile's great flood,
Has changed its waters into blood!
   A warning and a token
      Of plagues reserved
      For those who swerved,
      By power nerved,
      From laws humane,
      And dared constrain
God's witnesses to works **profane**!

3 The **clime** of darkness **blacker** grows,
No beam the worship'd sun-god throws
   Within the heathen's palace;
Regardless of **the** despot's prayer
Compell'd with trembling and with fear
   To **drain** the bitter chalice;
      Behold and praise
      God's wondrous ways
      Each hour displays!
      In con**trast** bright
      To Egypt's night
On Israel's home shines perfect light.

4 **And** thus with concentrated ray
On all who heaven's will obey,
   Whate'er may be their station,
Through all the shadows cast by time,
Shall rise in lustrous grace sublime
   The blest star of salvation!
      The tyrant's doom
      In midnight gloom,
      From throne to tomb
      On freedom's spot
      It resteth not:
Light to man's *spirit there* **is** brought.

5 Creator! Liberator! Lord!
Let peace to us its palm accord,
Twined with faith's pure evergreen
Oh! bless the rulers of each land,
Who cause its branches to expand,
Its rare fruitage to be seen.
Most holy King!
Let Judah cling
To laws that spring
From Mercy's seat,
While at Thy feet
This day's memorial we repeat.

199 Hallelujah! Praise to Thee,
Mighty God of victory!
Voice of Jacob, now repeat
Paschal anthems, loud and sweet.

2 Hallelujah! God hath bowed
Hearts idolatrous and proud—
Whelmed amid their vain career,
Courser, car, and charioteer!

3 Hallelujah! Let us sing,
Sound the trump, the timbrels ring!
Tyrant-kings shall never more
Scorn the God that we adore.

4 Hallelujah! Spear and shield
Vainly may the strongest wield;
Weak the cause that virtue wrongs,
Triumph but to truth belongs.

5 Hallelujah! Symbol bright
Of divine, impartial light
Is the sun that taketh heed
Of the flower and the weed.

6 Hallelujah! Even so
  Mercy beams on all below;
  Nor to saints its smiles confines,
  But on guilt forgiving shines.

7 Hallelujah! Full and free
  Swelled the Hebrews' choral glee,
  As to Palestine they sped,
  By the God of battles led.

8 Hallelujah! May our race,
  Heirs of promise and of grace,
  Enter heav'n beyond life's goal,
  Blessed Canaan of the soul!
                    HALLELUJAH!
                           P. M.

200 Glory to God! whose outstretched hand
  Hath smitten Pharaoh's mighty band.
  Let songs through all the tribes resound,
  Ransom for Israel hath been found,
  A refuge from the scourge and chain,
  A shield from the oppressor's reign.

2 The Red Sea is in triumph past;
  Praise to the Ruler of the blast!
  At whose strong breath the waves rolled by,
  And left the deep foundation dry.
  Behold the pride of Egypt checked,
  Her princes, priests, and warriors wrecked.

3 In vain to helpless gods they plead
  For succor in the hour of need;
  No providence like ours they know,
  To make the flood its prey forego.
  Rider and steed in terror sink,
  While Judah gains the desert's brink.

4 Sole King of heaven and earth! protect
　The residue of Thy elect!
　Let piety redeem their souls,
　Whom sin in fearful bondage holds!
　O Israel! hear her angel tone,
　And bow before **One God** alone!　　P. M.

201 Hallelujah!
　　Sing ever thus before the Lord,
　　O Israel! with one accord
　　　His name thus glorify;
　　Such tribute piety demands
　　From dwellers in the desert sands,
　　　And nations proud and high.
　　　　　　　　Hallelujah!

2 Hallelujah!
　　In battle, who shall be our shield?
　　By whom shall our wounds be healed,
　　　But Thee, O God supreme?
　　Saviour, in danger and distress,
　　Who can alone all wrongs redress,
　　　And man from sin redeem!
　　　　　　　　Hallelujah!

3 Hallelujah!
　　When before Judah's host He past,
　　Earth from its orb night's shadow cast,
　　　And brighter grew than day;
　　As changing to a golden cloud,
　　The moving columns dusky shroud,
　　　Unveiled His glory lay.
　　　　　　　　Hallelujah!

4 Hallelujah!
   On, on the holy standards flew,
   And victory the angel knew
     Whose light her course controls;
   And to the legions of the Lord
   Gave liberty—the blest reward
     Of their confiding souls.
                         Hallelujah!

5 Hallelujah!
   Woe to the courser **and** the car,
   Struggling to stem the liquid bar,
     That would their progress check;
   Woe **to** the prince, whose daring **band,**
   Braved *Him*, in whose almighty hand,
     Redemption **lies, and** wreck.
                         Hallelujah!

6 Hallelujah!
   And now from the triumphant **ranks**
   Sweet minstrels send m**e**lodious thanks
     To God, for ever near;
   Whose spirit like the **parting sun,**
   Smiled on the work itself **had done,**
     And left a glory there.
                         Hallelujah!

7 Hallelujah!
   When first **devotion**'s heart was stirred,
   It found a volume on this word,
     Dropt from a seraph's tongue;
   And, oh! when life is on the wane,
   By faith shall this celestial strain
     Be to man's spirit sung.
                         HALLELUJAH!
                                P. M.

7. PENTECOST.

202 Let us to prayer! it is the holy time,
When Moses stood on Sinai's mount sublime,
Communing with that uncreated One,
Whose glory on his brow reflected shone.

2 Earth reeled in presence of its mighty King,
From whom eternal truth and knowledge spring;
Red lightnings quivered o'er the conscious sod,
As man revealed the graven laws of God.

3 O house of Jacob! upon "eagles' wings"
Triumphant borne through desert wanderings;
Ye who have been the Lord's peculiar choice,
For ever in that covenant rejoice!

4 Oh! treasure until life itself departs
Those precious statutes in your inmost hearts!
Cause every member of your household band
Daily to meditate on each command;

5 Until the spirit of those words divine,
Sheds on their souls its influence benign!
Blessing and curse are both before ye set,
May ye the promise win, and ward the threat!

P. M.

203
Rejoice in God, our mighty Rock,
 Whose promise, blissful and sublime,
Intrusted to his chosen flock,
 Will be fulfilled in future time,
And Israel with glory crown'd,
 Shall sanctify His holy Name;
His doctrines pure and truths profound
 All earth will then with joy proclaim.

2 "Of nations be thou mine elect,
 A priestly kingdom unto me;
Within thy midst the fane erect
 Of light, and truth, and charity.
My spirit then will ever rest
 On thee, the people of my heart;
My word, our covenant's behest,
 Will never from thy race depart!"

3 Thou hast, O Father! faithfully
 Kept that paternal covenant,
Protected 'gainst calamity
 And cruel scorn Thy chosen band.
Hast been with them, where'er they dwelt,
 And hearkened, when from bitter grief
Before Thine altar down they knelt,
 To supplicate Thee for relief.

4 Again we now before Thee stand,
 O God of old! with festal glee;
Free children of a glorious land
 The covenant renew with Thee.
For tho' deep error's heavy guilt
 Rests yet upon our heart and soul,
Thy word's inheritance Thou wilt
 That we should guard to life's last goal.

5 And when religion's victory
   Will all the earth have sanctified,
 The heav'nly rule of charity
   The hearts of mankind purified :—
 Then will all o'er the world resound
   Again that holy, awful word,
 Proclaimed to us on Sinai's mount :
   "*I am th' Eternal God, thy Lord !*"

6. And into ONE great brotherhood
    That call the human race will turn ;
  To know Thee to be just and good,
    And love each other they will learn.
  The patient lamb and quiet sheep,
    With wolves and lions strong will play ;
  And heav'nly peace, serene and deep,
    Will shed on earth its blissful ray.

7 And all will worship Thee alone,
    Our sole Redeemer, God, and Lord !
  Contention will no more be known
    On earth, enlightened by Thy word.
  All men, inspired by truth and love,
    With one accord will then exclaim :
  "The Lord is ONE in heav'n above,
    And ONE on earth His glorious Name !"

M. M.

204 We bring not to our holy shrine,
     Gath'rings like those of Palestine ;
     No golden sheaves, or olives green,
     Or clustering grapes may there be seen ;

  2 No harvest-song is heard to swell,
     Where Hebrews in their exile dwell ;
     Yet mourn not Israel for this,
     Bring ye the fruits of righteousness !

3 Cultivate virtue's holy ground,
   Where pure philanthropy is found;
   That human vine which in its folds,
   With loving clasp its neighbor holds.

4 Let peace its palmy branches spread,
   And charity its balm-drops shed;
   Meek faith unto the altar bring,
   And tears for trespass-offering.

5 Fruits of the spirit consecrate
   To God, supremely wise and great;
   Reapers of grace shall ye then be
   In fields of immortality.   P. M.

VIII. CONFIRMATION HYMNS.

205 God! to my spirit's great delight,
   I Thy law in childhood learned,
When faith towards my wondering sight,
   Thine eternal tablets turned;
Showing with what abundant grace,
   Father! Thou with hand divine
Didst those great testimonies trace,
   Which now mark man's moral line.

2 Young are the lips that venture now,
   In thy gracious presence, Lord!
To pronounce the solemn vow,
   Listening angels will record;
Yet firmly, freely we respond
   Unto piety's appeal,
Now to take on us the bond,
   Under confirmation's seal!

3 As members enter Israel's fold,
    With consent of heart and mind,
In fellowship of faith enrolled,
    Until life shall be resigned;
In every clime beneath the sun,
Loudly will we e'er proclaim,
That the Lord our God is *One!*
    And adore *His* holy name.

4 Heavenly Sire! watchers station
    O'er the wavering and the weak,
Who the meshes of temptation,
    Have not strength enough to break;
Oh! let not sin, (an infant yet
    At the threshold of the soul,)
There mature, decoys to set,
    All its movements to control.

5 Guide of innocence! direct us
    Onward to salvation's road,
From those passions still protect us,
    Which e'en youthful hearts corrode.
Links of love let us not sever,
    By rude strife or wrathful words;
But unite in kind endeavor,
    Closer still to bind its chords.

6 Thou sendest angels pure to guard
    The cradles by our mother rocked,
These *first* the gates of truth unbarred,
    And with these in prayer we talked.
And when in earth's last cradle set,
    The trembling soul would heav'n reach,
These as its holy guardians yet
    Shall the young immortal teach.   P. M.

206   Happy he whom nature mouldeth,
    Virtue's impress to receive,—
Whom her moral law upholdeth,
    And will to her practice cleave.

2 Happy he who seeks promotion
    Only where *her* ranks are found :
Disciplined by true devotion,
    Fearlessly to tread her ground.

3 Happy he who, young and tender,
    Enters piety's abode ;
Prayers to breathe, and praises render,
    For the gifts by God bestow'd.

4 Happy he who as his preacher
    Hath that angel from above,
Frailty's most indulgent teacher ;
    Blessed, pure, benignant love ;

5 Who as Mercy's envoy meekly
    Judges young transgressors here,
In unguarded moments weakly
    Drawn into corruption's sphere ;

6 Who, when earthly parents perish,
    Tidings to the orphan brings :
God the fatherless will cherish
    'Neath the shadow of His wings.

7 Happy he who humbly hearkens
    To religion's voice in youth,
That when time his prospect darkens,
    Cheers him with the beams of truth.

8 Turn then, O ye young and careless !
    Leave awhile your sports, to learn
Laws to which, in seasons cheerless,
    Ye for light and warmth may turn :

9 Precepts that shall overpower
    Peril, poverty, and pain,
Such as in the last dread hour,
    Victory o'er death shall gain!

10 Faith on her erring children calleth,
    God's forgiveness to implore;
Promising each tear that falleth,
    Ransom shall for sin procure.   P. M.

207 God of my fathers! in Thy sight
    With reverential awe, I vow
To be confirmed an Israelite,
    And only at *Thy* altar bow.
Merciful Lord! with grief intense,
    I think, how often when a child,
The paradise of innocence
    Was by my passions rude defiled.

2 Oft did my wayward spirit break
    The prime injunction of Thy law,
And for some worthless idol's sake,
    Its worship from Thyself withdraw.
And, oh! tho' from Thy holy book
    Another text was daily read,
Vainly Thy sacred name I took,
    By levity or anger led.

3 Blest Sabbath! nature's golden hours,
    Holy, sanctified, serene,
When children yet with youthful pow'rs,
    The fruits of godliness should glean,
No incense from that little urn,
    Where infant life its spark secretes,
Was brought before *Thy* shrine to burn,
    Whose bounty lavished countless sweets.

4 Nor, though an angel's voice might call
    For silence in the house of pray'r,
And show the writing on the wall:
    "Know before whom thou standest here!"
From idle converse would I pause;
    Regardless of paternal threats
'Gainst those who coldly serve Thy cause,
    I failed to pay my filial debts.

5 Remembrance now my soul alarms,
    By bringing back in sad review,
The guardians to whose fost'ring arms
    In suff'ring I, or sorrow flew,
Wounded by my rebellious ways,
    Infringing on that great command:
"Honor thy parents, that thy days
    Be long and happy in the land."

6 "Thou shalt not covet!" Woe is me!
    Forgetful of that charge divine,
Not without envy could I see
    A neighbor's gift excelling mine!
O gracious God! dare I then stand
    Before Thee as a candidate
For place among the chosen band,
    Who shall Thy law perpetuate?

7 But hark! A seraph whispers now:
    "Courage! and from thy sins depart!
God will accept thy contrite vow,
    And make thee of His fold a part.
Be thou a Hebrew, sanctified,
    His Unity to promulgate,
Nor, tho' dissenting brothers chide,
    From thy great purpose deviate.

S "In Providence then firmly trust,
   E'en when it seemeth *most* to frown;
It raiseth meekness *from* the dust,
   And *to* it brings the haughty down.
God's promise reacheth to the tomb,
   Whence righteous spirits shall migrate,
Immortal graces to assume,
   And all His glory contemplate."   P. M.

APPENDIX.

SCHOOL HYMNS.

208 Oh! fill our hearts, Almighty King!
    With gratitude to Thee,
That we Thy praise may gladly sing,
    In all humility.

2 May we instruction now receive,
    With willing heart and mind,
And all Thy laws, O God! believe,
    Who art so just and kind;

3 Who watchest o'er our actions here,
    And guardest us from ill;
Oh! teach us humbly to revere,
    And bow before Thy will.

4 And when our souls thou callest hence
    To life beyond the tomb,
May there our youth we recommence,
    For everlasting bloom.

209 With grateful hearts of song and praise
And filial love to Thee we raise,
For all that Thou hast ever done
For us, Thy children, holy One!

2 To Thee our life and health we owe,
And ev'ry competence below;
Our soul immortal thou hast given,
To dwell again with Thee in heaven.

3 Our tender age by parents dear
　Is watched with never-tiring care;
　May we with joyful willingness
　Their counsels on our hearts impress!

4 Our teachers, true in deed and word,
　Instruct us in Thy law, O Lord!
　May we this law before us set,
　And their monitions ne'er forget!

5 Do Thou assist us, while we strive
　On earth with all in peace to live;
　And grant us, after death, O King!
　With angels joined, Thy praise to sing!
M. M.

210 Almighty God! we pray to Thee,
　　　To lead us with paternal hand,
　　In paths of truth and piety;
　　　And teach us well to understand,
　　Tho' young in years, Thy holy will,
　　And all our duties to fulfill.

2 Bestow Thy blessing, holy Lord!
　　On those who, with untiring zeal,
　Teach us Thine everlasting word:
　　A guide through life, in woe and weal,
　A shield against the snares of sin,
　A help Thy pleasure e'er to win.

3 May we in wisdom, Lord! progress—
　　By daily practice ever show
　That truly we *Thy* law profess,
　　And strive by all our toils below,
　To gain, at last, the choicest prize—
　Eternal bliss beyond the skies.
M. M.

PSALM OF DAVID.

MEEZEMORE.

Haboo ladonai banà-aleem, haboo ladonai kabode va-ngoze, Haboo ladonai kabode shamo, hishta-chàvva ladonai ba-hadrat Kodesh. Kole adonai ngal-hamàyeem ale-chá-kábode hir-ngeem adonai ngal màyeem-rábeem. Kole àdonai bà-koach kole ádonai ba-hádár. Kole adonai shobare arä-zeem, va-isha-bare e-tar-za ha-la-banon va-yar-kedame kamo ngaguel labanon va shuryon kamo ben-rai-ameme. Kole adonai chotsabe làhabote ashe. Kole adonai ya-cheel midbar, yacheel àdonai midbar kadoshe, kole adonai ya-cho-lale aya-lote, vasofe yangarote oob-hachalo, koolo omáre kabode. Ádonai lá-mábule yasheb vayasheb ádonai malech langolam ádonai ngose la-ngamo-yetane adonai yabà-rach etngnamo bá-shá-lome.

AH-DO-NGO-LAM

Ah-do-ngo-lam à-share malach ba-ta-rem
Kol yet-sar neeb-ra,
Langet nang-sa Kaheftsokol àizài
Malech sha-mo-nikra,
Và áchare-kick tohhakol labàdo yeemloch nora.
Vahàhàyoh vahohova vehuyeya bateefarà,

Vahooachad va-enshène lahamshelo la-achberà
Balerashete, balatochlete valoàngoze và-àmeesrà,
Balingnerech, baledimjone, baleshenoo ve-atmurah,
Balechebure, baleferood, gadole-koach vahàgaboorà,

Vahoo-ale vachà-go-àle vatzoor cheeble bayome tza-rah,
Vahoonesee hoo-mà-noose manet-kosee bayome ek-rah.

Bayàdo afkeed roo-che bengeteshan ve-angerah,
Beyimruche gaveyàtee adonai le valoerà.

YIGDAL.

Yigdal alohimchà vayish ta-bach
Neem-tzar ve-a-ngnet-el ma-tze oo to,
Echad vaaneya chid kayehudo,
Nanglam vagain en suf la ach dooto.
Enlo damoot hà goof va a noo goof,
Lo na ngarach alan Kadooshàto,
Kodmone lachal dabar à sher neebrà,
Rashone va ane rasheet larash-e-toh.
Eno adone ngolam lachol notzar,
Yora gadoolàto hoomalchuto.
Shafang nabooàtoh natango-ale,
Ansha sagoolato vateefàr-to
Lokam bayisràel kamosha-ngode,
Nabi oomàbeetel tamoo-nàto,
Torat amet nàtan langàmoel,
Ngalyad nabeo ahman-bato.
Loyar hà-lef-àel valo-yàmcer dàto
Langolàmim lazulàto
Tsofa vayoda-ang sà-tàra-noo
Mabeet lasofe dàbar bechad-mooto.
Gomel la-ish chaseed kamif-ngàto
Noten larashangrang kareesh-ngàto.
Yeeshlach lakaatz-yamim mashechanoo
Lifdote machàka-kaatz yàshoo-ngàto.

Mateem yacháyahel **barobe** chasdo,
Baruch ngad dangad shem táelàto.
Aìa shalosh ngesra laneek rãneem
Enam yasodàtel vatoràto.
  (*Repeat Matcem.*)

ANE-KA-LO-HA-NOO.

1 **Anekalohanoo,** Anekàdonanu,
  Anekamalkanoo, Anekamo sheenganoo,
  Mekalohanoo, Mekádonanoo,
  Mekamalkanoo, Mekamoshenganoo.

2 **No**dalolahanoo, **No**dalàdonanoo,
  Nodalamalkanoo, Nodalamo-shenganoo,
  Baruch alohanoo, Baruch **à**donanoo
  Baruch Malkanoo Baruch **mos**henganoo.

3 Àtà oolohanoo, Àtà oolàdonanoo,
  Àtà oomalkanoo, Àtà oomoshenganoo,
  Àtà toshengano, Àtà takoom tarà
  Chemtzeyone **kenget lahenngenà kebà monged**.

www.ingramcontent.com/pod-product-compliance
Lightning Source LLC
Chambersburg PA
CBHW021842230426
43669CB00008B/1053